First Published in the UK in 2014 by Focus Education (UK) Ltd
Updated in September 2014
Updated January 2018

Focus Education (UK) Ltd
Publishing
Talking Point
Huddersfield Road
Scouthead
Saddleworth
OL4 4AG

Focus Education (UK) Ltd Reg. No 4507968
ISBN 978-1-909038-29-5

www.focus-education.co.uk
customerservice@focus-education.co.uk
Printed in Great Britain by Focus Education UK Ltd,
Scouthead

About the Author

Ros Ferrara is a full-time consultant with Focus Education.

Prior to joining Focus, Ros worked in a consultancy and advisory role for Lambeth LA. During this period, she led development work on the National Strategies highly successful EAL Programme, was the Literacy lead for the authority and Primary Strategy Manager. Ros led and managed a range of initiatives, including Every Child a Reader, Every Child a Writer and action research aimed at improving writing. Her role also involved working very closely with senior leaders in schools on developing leadership, improving the quality of teaching and other school improvement issues.

Following this, Ros led a buy-back school improvement service out of a Federation of schools.

She is also an accredited additional inspector with Tribal and continues to undertake inspections.

Recent feedback:

Very professional: we had confidence in her judgements.
Style was relaxed and approachable. Good balance between listening and practical activities.
Ros was wonderful. The material was relevant and interesting. Ros's presentation skills were excellent. Her interactions with teachers were professional but relaxed.
Ros has transformed writing in the school. The support received both by senior leaders, middle managers and classroom practitioners has been key to our becoming an outstanding school.
The consultancy Ros has given to my school has empowered my staff and the impact is already notable when I look at pupil outcomes.

Contents

INTRODUCTION
USING A QUALITY TEXT TO INSPIRE WRITING

Books chosen to inspire writing must be of high quality – a book must be worth talking about!

A text can be used as the core for a Literacy unit of work as well as an explicit link to other curriculum areas. It is important to know the texts used well.

The following should always be considered:

- Will this text help move learning on?
- How could this text be used to target the need in the class?
- Which skills/objectives from the year group will be needed?
- What activities could be planned?

The activities must provide the key learning and skills which the children need for the identified outcome.

Using the Planning from Quality Texts Menus

These documents are intended to support the planning of effective literacy units based on high quality books. They are not intended to be lesson plans, but offer a menu of ***possible*** ideas for teachers to use as ***starting*** points to plan for purposeful learning and give pupils reasons for writing as well as the skills they need to write with impact on their reader. They follow a learning sequence:

- a hook to fully engage and interest the children
- responding to reading activities to allow immersion in and exploration of the text, including picture exploration, book and writer talk
- capturing ideas activities which include drama and talk to support understanding of the text and to develop vocabulary, language and ideas for writing
- possibilities for the contextualised teaching of grammar
- sentence games to develop creativity, vocabulary, language and grammar
- links to guided reading
- a range of writing tasks which may be final unit outcomes or incidental opportunities during the unit

Specific objectives are not included as they will need to be identified by teachers based on on-going assessment from prior units and the particular skills needed for pupils to achieve the identified outcome.

Responding to a Text

Book Talk

Explore both written text and illustrations.
Consider likes, dislikes, questions and reminders.
Explore characters, settings, plot.

Writer Talk

Consider how text is structured.
Look at the sentences the writer has used.
What is the effect?
How has the writer created impact?
Drama, speaking and listening activities

Capturing Ideas

Develop ideas for written outcome –
Vocabulary exploration and development
Develop changes to character, setting, plot
Role play activities
Research information
Planning

Contextualised Grammar Teaching

Developing a repertoire of skills

Identify the grammar needed for the outcome.
Build in language play.
Focus on using grammar to create effects to impact on the reader.
Building a writer's toolkit
Oral rehearsal of sentences.

Writing Process

Modelled writing
Shared writing
Guided writing
Independent writing

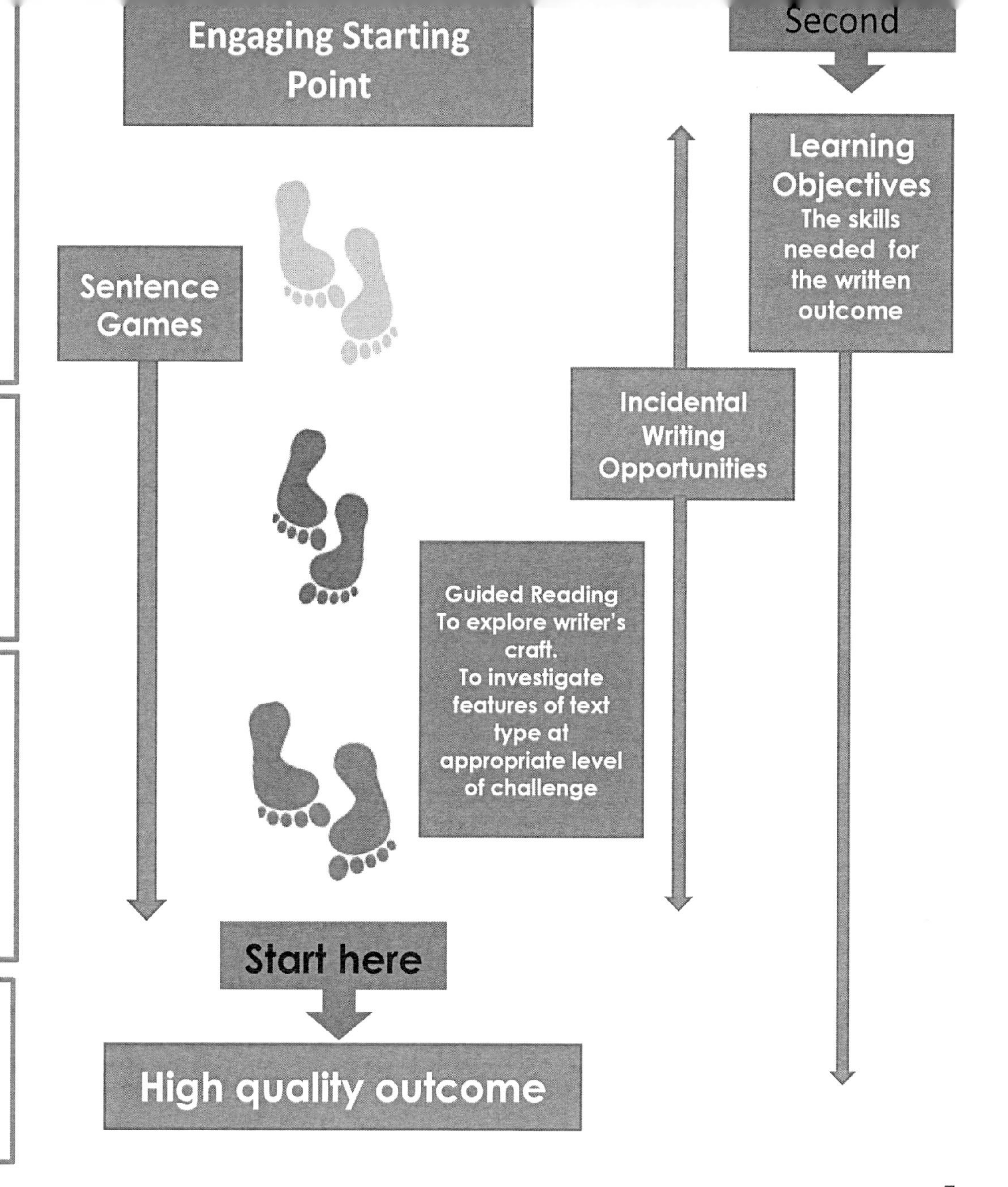

The Planning Process

Step 1

Decide on the final written or oral outcome for the unit of work.

Step 2

Based on the skills the children will need to successfully achieve the outcome and formative assessment information from the previous unit and cross-curricular work, identify the objectives to be covered. Bear in mind how these will need to be differentiated to meet different needs. These will include the grammatical features and structures that will need to be used in the final outcome.

Step 3

Think of additional incidental writing opportunities which can be built in to the unit to make sure that pupils have enough opportunities to write.

Step 4

Identify books or reading materials to be used for guided reading.

Step 5

Plan in some sentence games. These may be to reinforce prior learning, consolidate learning, experiment with sentences and vocabulary or develop creativity.

Step 6

Plan activities to allow children to become immersed in and respond to the text being used based on the objectives identified. These will include speaking and listening and drama activities and oral retelling. Identify activities to support the children reading as writers and understanding how the writer has created impact. These may include looking at how a text is structured overall, how a writer has used sentences and grammatical features and how the writer has made word choices.

Step 7

Keeping in mind the identified objectives, plan activities to develop children's ideas for the outcome. This may also include speaking and listening and drama as well as research.

Step 8

Plan in opportunities for the teaching of the grammar needed. Opportunities for pupils to experiment with different structures and vocabulary are essential. All activities here should be contextualised and draw on the ideas developed so that the focus is on the grammar and not generating ideas. Plan in specific opportunities for oral rehearsal of sentences and sequences of sentences.

The Writing Sequence

Modelled Writing

Teacher models the writing process aloud and the decisions writers make about sentences, paragraphs etc. to create impact on the reader. This can also include the modelling of planning and spelling strategies.

Shared Writing

Collaborative composition with discussion and suggestions about what to write and how to write it to create the intended effect. At this point children may write a sentence/s, often in pairs, on whiteboards which are then discussed.

Guided Writing

Small group sessions based on specific needs of a specific group of children. The session may address misconceptions, bridge gaps or extend learning and can take place at any point during the unit.

Text Selection

Many of the books selected may be used across the school with year groups. The menus are designed to offer opportunities for flexible different use as appropriate. They indicate a possible key stage, a range of year groups or a specific year group. This does not preclude their adaptation and use in other contexts.

EYFS MENUS

EYFS MENUS

BOOK TITLE	PHASE / YEAR GROUP	PAGE
Bedtime for Monsters	EYFS	14
Billy's Bucket	EYFS	17
Elmer	EYFS	20
Knuffle Bunny	EYFS	23
Oi! Get off our Train	EYFS	26
Penguin	EYFS	29
The Acorn	EYFS	32
The Tiger who Came to Tea	EYFS	35
Whatever Next!	EYFS	38
Where the Wild Things Are	EYFS	41

Planning for Quality Texts EYFS: Bedtime for Monsters

These documents are intended to support the planning of effective literacy units based on high quality books. They are not intended to be lesson plans, but offer a menu of possible ideas for teachers to use as starting points to plan for purposeful learning and give pupils reasons for writing as well as the skills they need to write with impact on their reader. They follow a learning sequence:

- a hook to fully engage and interest the children
- responding to reading activities to allow immersion in and exploration of the text, including picture exploration, book and writer talk
- capturing ideas activities which include drama and talk to support understanding of the text and to develop vocabulary, language and ideas for writing
- activities focused on the development of spoken language and vocabulary development
- sentence games to develop creativity and the understanding of the concept of a sentence
- links to guided reading
- a range of writing tasks which may be guided in a focus group or incidental opportunities both in and outside the classroom

Specific mention is made of the writing sequence:

- modelled writing - teacher models the writing process aloud and the decisions writers make about sentences and word choices to create impact on the reader. This can also include the modelling of oral rehearsal of sentences and application of phonic learning.
- shared writing - collaborative composition with discussion and suggestions about what to write and how to write it to create the intended effect. At this point children may write a sentence/s, often in pairs, on whiteboards which are then discussed.
- guided writing - small group sessions based on specific needs of a specific group of children. The session may address misconceptions, bridge gaps or extend learning and can take place at any point during the unit.

In addition, cross-curricular links are suggested, including links to challenges from the Learning Challenge Curriculum.

Possible Written/Spoken Outcomes or Incidental Writing/Speaking Opportunities

- Retell story using map
- Draw monster from book and label or write caption
- Create own monster and label or write caption
- Thought bubble/speech bubble for monster - written or recorded
- Make bedtime routine
- Recommend a favourite story and say why you recommend it
- Tell monster a bedtime story
- Draw different place where the monster might travel
- Add label/caption /sentence
- Monster-shaped paper/books to write your own bedtime story in writing area
- Flap book to draw/write night time fears and what makes them feel safe

EYFS

Hook

- Photocopy and laminate different monsters from second page and hide. Go on a monster hunt.
- Monster footprints in flour across room/ monster prints in sand tray/ mud kitchen etc

1. Responding to the Text

- Book talk: Prediction - Use picture from front cover without title. Who is this? What do you think it is thinking about?
- Book talk: Can you find any clues that tell you if the monster is nice or nasty?
- Book talk: Can you find all the places that the monster travels through on his journey?
- Book talk: Prediction - stop at page where monster is opening the door. What do you think it is going to do?
- Book talk: Were you surprised by the ending? Can you say why?
- Book talk: What clues can you find in the last pages that tell us that the monster is nice?
- Book talk: Which part of the book do you like best? Can you say why?
- Book talk: Have you got any questions you would like to ask the monster?
- Book talk: Do you know any other stories about monsters?
- Writer talk: Can you find the words that tell us about sounds in the story?

2. Capturing Ideas

- Set up journey monster makes outside using available resources - for example bicycle, muddy area, willow tunnel
- Create journey environments in tuff spots
- Story map journey
- Retell story with focus on sounds and sequence using map
- Role play story as the monster using route or tuff spot
- The monster was licking his lips. What makes you lick your lips?
- How did the monster feel at each part of his journey? What might he have thought? What might he have said?
- Favourite bedtime stories
- What might be a monster's favourite bedtime story?
- Use musical instruments/body percussion to add to story
- Other places that the monster might have travelled - desert, river, tall grass

Sentence Games (use throughout unit)

- Sentence not a sentence game based on book
- Chain writing with a focus on creating accurate sentence with noun, adjective and verb
- Sound sort/Detective linked to current phonic learning

Guided Reading Possibilities

- Explore Bedtime for Monsters in detail - opportunities to look at illustrations as well as responding to and discussing book.
- Compare to We're Going on a Bear Hunt
- Rhymes/Lullabies - Twinkle, Twinkle Little Star/Rock-a-Bye Baby

Spoken Language

- Responding to questions in full sentences - responses should be clearly modelled. For example - My favourite story is… I like it because…
- Develop vocabulary - sound words and words to describe monster
- Learn lullaby or bedtime song
- Thinking of questions to ask the monster

Modelled Writing
Shared Writing
Guided Writing
Independent Writing

MAKING LINKS ACROSS THE CURRICULUM

Knowledge and Understanding of the World
- Mapping monster's journey
- Different environments - forest, mountain, swamp etc

Maths
- 3-D shapes for monster models
- Times of day

ICT
- Have video of story available for children to access
- Compare with clip from Monsters INC

PSED
- Bedtime routines
- Making links with own experiences - does the monster want the same things at bedtime as we do?
- Are you afraid of anything at night? What makes you feel safe?

Useful links
https://www.youtube.com/watch?v=5JdAh8OOMVs
https://www.youtube.com/watch?v=vMOLjKAuqyA
https://www.youtube.com/watch?v=2OAwz0A0Z6w

Creative Development
- Making own monsters - 3-D to use to re-create journey in tuff spot
- Make new environment using natural materials
- Paint/draw monsters

Year N: What makes a sound?

The Learning Challenge CURRICULUM

Author: Ed Vere
Publisher: Puffin Books
ISBN- 13:978-0141502397

Planning for Quality Texts EYFS: Billy's Bucket

These documents are intended to support the planning of effective literacy units based on high quality books. They are not intended to be lesson plans, but offer a menu of possible ideas for teachers to use as starting points to plan for purposeful learning and give pupils reasons for writing as well as the skills they need to write with impact on their reader. They follow a learning sequence:

- a hook to fully engage and interest the children
- responding to reading activities to allow immersion in and exploration of the text, including picture exploration, book and writer talk
- capturing ideas activities which include drama and talk to support understanding of the text and to develop vocabulary, language and ideas for writing
- activities focused on the development of spoken language and vocabulary development
- sentence games to develop creativity and the understanding of the concept of a sentence
- links to guided reading
- a range of writing tasks which may be guided in a focus group or incidental opportunities both in and outside the classroom

Specific mention is made of the writing sequence:

- modelled writing - teacher models the writing process aloud and the decisions writers make about sentences and word choices to create impact on the reader. This can also include the modelling of oral rehearsal of sentences and application of phonic learning.
- shared writing - collaborative composition with discussion and suggestions about what to write and how to write it to create the intended effect. At this point children may write a sentence/s, often in pairs, on whiteboards which are then discussed.
- guided writing - small group sessions based on specific needs of a specific group of children. The session may address misconceptions, bridge gaps or extend learning and can take place at any point during the unit.

In addition, cross-curricular links are suggested, including links to challenges from the Learning Challenge Curriculum.

Possible Written/Spoken Outcomes or Incidental Writing/Speaking Opportunities

- Label for bucket
- Warning sign for bucket
- Birthday list
- Labels, price tags, signs, notices, receipts for shop
- Bucket shaped books for writing and drawing the creatures found in Billy's Bucket
- Zigzag book to retell story
- Bucket shaped book for different bucket - farm bucket, football bucket - to draw/write what the contents might be
- Lift the flap book to show what could be in a bucket
- Question and answer speech bubbles from model in book - What's in your bucket now Billy? etc.
- Labelled picture/fact file on sea creature
- Poster for aquarium
- Ticket for aquarium

EYFS

Hook

- Set up Buckets R Us shop with a collection of buckets for children to discover
- Visit to an aquarium

1. Responding to the Text

- Book talk: Why do you think Billy wanted a bucket for his birthday?
- Book talk: Did Billy know the bucket was special? How did he know?
- Book talk: Why didn't Billy's parents believe that he had the things he told them were in his bucket?
- Book talk: How could the sea creatures have got into the bucket?
- Book talk: Should Billy's parents have borrowed his bucket?
- Book talk: Why didn't Billy want his parents to borrow his bucket?
- Book talk: Which part of the book do you like best? Can you say why?
- Book talk: Have you got any questions you would like to ask Billy or his parents?
- Writer talk: What do you notice about how some of the words are written?
- Writer talk: What do you notice about how some of the sentences are written on the pages?

2. Capturing Ideas

- Role play area set up as Buckets R Us shop
- Water tray with sea creatures from story
- Matching labels to pictures or small world resources of creatures from story
- Create story about sea creatures in tray
- Make picture sequence or story map
- Retell story orally from picture sequence or story map
- Children bring buckets from home
- What do we use buckets for? Who uses them?
- Have range of buckets for different uses - farm, football from story
- Have range of buckets and decide their use and what might be found in them
- What would you like to find in your bucket?
- Role play question and answer model from story - original text and own bucket
- Investigate the different sea creatures in the story and those to be found in an aquarium

Sentence Games (use throughout unit)

- Sentence not a sentence game based on book
- Chain writing with a focus on creating accurate sentence with noun, adjective and verb
- Use rhyme 12345 Once I Caught a Fish Alive and change with other sea creatures - crab, whale etc.
- Sound sort/Detective linked to current phonic learning

Guided Reading Possibilities

- Explore Billy's Bucket in detail - opportunities to look at cartoon like illustrations and angles as well as responding to and discussing book.
- Non-fiction books about sea creatures and underwater life
- Seaside Poems - Jill Bennett

Spoken Language

- Responding to questions in full sentences - responses should be clearly modelled. For example - In my bucket I would find...
- Role play/Rehearsal of question and answer model from book
- Learn and recite 12345 Once I Caught a Fish Alive
- Use related songs and rhymes - Jack and Jill, There's a Hole in my Bucket etc.
- Model problem -solving language - you could...., if i... the bucket will...

Modelled Writing
Shared Writing
Guided Writing
Independent Writing

MAKING LINKS ACROSS THE CURRICULUM

Knowledge and Understanding of the World

- Different sea creatures
- Set up aquarium
- Explain that some of the buckets need to be moved. For example - raised high or a heavy bucket to be moved across the outdoor area. Problem-solving activity.
- What are buckets made of?

Maths

- Cost of buckets - buying and selling in shop
- Counting numbers of creatures in bucket using book and small world resources
- Ordering sea creatures in size - use of language big, bigger etc.
- Comparative mathematical language - The angel fish is smaller than the dolphin etc

ICT

- Have video of story available for children to access
- Look for information and pictures of sea creatures
-

PSED

- Working together to solve problems
- Making links with own experiences

Useful links

https://www.youtube.com/watch?v=GJOszyHKjMk

Creative Development

- Designs for buckets for Buckets R Us
- Create an underwater scene collage
- Make tanks and sea creatures for aquarium

Nursery:What can I do with water?

The Learning Challenge CURRICULUM

Author: Kes Gray
Publisher: Red Fox
ISBN- 13: 978-0099438748

Planning for Quality Texts EYFS: Elmer

These documents are intended to support the planning of effective literacy units based on high quality books. They are not intended to be lesson plans, but offer a menu of possible ideas for teachers to use as starting points to plan for purposeful learning and give pupils reasons for writing as well as the skills they need to write with impact on their reader. They follow a learning sequence:

- a hook to fully engage and interest the children
- responding to reading activities to allow immersion in and exploration of the text, including picture exploration, book and writer talk
- capturing ideas activities which include drama and talk to support understanding of the text and to develop vocabulary, language and ideas for writing
- activities focused on the development of spoken language and vocabulary development
- sentence games to develop creativity and the understanding of the concept of a sentence
- links to guided reading
- a range of writing tasks which may be guided in a focus group or incidental opportunities both in and outside the classroom

Specific mention is made of the writing sequence:

- modelled writing - teacher models the writing process aloud and the decisions writers make about sentences and word choices to create impact on the reader. This can also include the modelling of oral rehearsal of sentences and application of phonic learning.
- shared writing - collaborative composition with discussion and suggestions about what to write and how to write it to create the intended effect. At this point children may write a sentence/s, often in pairs, on whiteboards which are then discussed.
- guided writing - small group sessions based on specific needs of a specific group of children. The session may address misconceptions, bridge gaps or extend learning and can take place at any point during the unit.

In addition, cross-curricular links are suggested, including links to challenges from the Learning Challenge Curriculum.

Possible Written/Spoken Outcomes or Incidental Writing/Speaking Opportunities

- Elephant shaped paper in Elmer colours
- Thought bubbles for Elmer and other elephants
- Speech bubbles for Elmer and other elephants
- Pictures of different kinds of elephants/elephant expression with caption or label
- Invitation to Elmer Day
- List of acceptances
- Questions - what would I like to find out about elephants?
- Label an elephant - tusks, trunk etc.
- Information about elephants
- Pictures/drawings of coloured objects/signs etc. in the environment
- Sign or object from environment - No Entry, Exit etc. for outside area - roadway etc
- Paint different greetings to Elmer on large stones to be placed outside

EYFS

Hook

- Coloured and grey elephant footprints across the room
- Letter from Elmer asking for help in organising an Elmer Day

1. Responding to the Text

- Book talk: Prediction - What might the story be about?
- Book talk: Why did Elmer feel different?
- Book talk: Do you think Elmer is beautiful?
- Book talk: Why did Elmer want to be like all the other elephants?
- Book talk: What happened when Elmer looked like all the other elephants?
- Book talk: How did the elephants treat Elmer when he looked the same as them?
- Book talk: What was the best joke Elmer ever played?
- Book talk: Which part of the book do you like best? Can you say why?
- Book talk: Do you think the grey elephants all looked exactly the same?
- Book talk: Do you know any other stories about elephants?
- Book talk: Can you think of anything you would like to ask Elmer?
- Writer talk: Can you find some adjectives that tell us about the different elephants?

2. Capturing Ideas

- Rainbow sand tray
- Elephant song(see video link)
- Make a giant spider web and investigate how many elephants it can hold. Try different materials to create web
- Favourite colours
- Colours that give us messages - red=danger etc.
- Colour hunt - coloured strips of card hidden and specific colours searched for
- Coloured objects buried in sand - dig for particular colours
- Small world jungle created in sand pit
- Retell story using small world jungle
- Plan and hold an Elmer day
- Make square biscuits and ice them like patchwork squares
- Explore how the elephants felt at different times in the story. What were they thinking? What were they saying?

Sentence Games (use throughout unit)

- Sentence not a sentence game based on book
- Chain writing with a focus on creating accurate sentence with noun, adjective and verb
- Adjectives that have talent to tell the reader how a character is feeling

Guided Reading Possibilities

- Explore Elmer in detail - opportunities to look at illustrations as well as responding to and discussing book.
- Read non-fiction texts about elephants
- Read other Elmer stories

Spoken Language

- Responding to questions in full sentences - responses should be clearly modelled. For example - I think Elmer is beautiful because..., I like the part when...best, I know a story called... about elephants.
- Oral retell of story with focus on key narrative language - there was once, when, as, after, after a while, finally etc.
- Spot the difference barrier game of elephant pictures

Modelled Writing
Shared Writing
Guided Writing
Independent Writing

MAKING LINKS ACROSS THE CURRICULUM

Knowledge and Understanding of the World
- Finding out about elephants
- Understanding the significance of specific colours in the environment
-

Maths
- Matching elephants with different patterns
- Following a sequence of coloured/patterned elephants
- Patterns with squares
- Counting - Elephant Song

ICT
- Make patterns with squares
- Dazzle to create pictures/patterns

PSED
- How to be a good friend
- What makes you special?

Useful links
https://www.youtube.com/watch?v=CP5uJVpHrVw
https://www.youtube.com/watch?v=qQHeyPi5fIA

Creative Development
- Colour mixing
- Elephant mask with moving trunk
- Printing with square sponges
- Junk model elephants

Nursery: Which colours make you feel happy and sad?
Year R: What do I know about me?

The Learning Challenge
CURRICULUM

Author: David McKee
Publisher: Red Fox
ISBN- 978-1842707319

Planning for Quality Texts EYFS: Knuffle Bunny

These documents are intended to support the planning of effective literacy units based on high quality books. They are not intended to be lesson plans, but offer a menu of possible ideas for teachers to use as starting points to plan for purposeful learning and give pupils reasons for writing as well as the skills they need to write with impact on their reader. They follow a learning sequence:

- a hook to fully engage and interest the children
- responding to reading activities to allow immersion in and exploration of the text, including picture exploration, book and writer talk
- capturing ideas activities which include drama and talk to support understanding of the text and to develop vocabulary, language and ideas for writing
- activities focused on the development of spoken language and vocabulary development
- sentence games to develop creativity and the understanding of the concept of a sentence
- links to guided reading
- a range of writing tasks which may be guided in a focus group or incidental opportunities both in and outside the classroom

Specific mention is made of the writing sequence:

- modelled writing - teacher models the writing process aloud and the decisions writers make about sentences and word choices to create impact on the reader. This can also include the modelling of oral rehearsal of sentences and application of phonic learning.
- shared writing - collaborative composition with discussion and suggestions about what to write and how to write it to create the intended effect. At this point children may write a sentence/s, often in pairs, on whiteboards which are then discussed.
- guided writing - small group sessions based on specific needs of a specific group of children. The session may address misconceptions, bridge gaps or extend learning and can take place at any point during the unit.

In addition, cross-curricular links are suggested, including links to challenges from the Learning Challenge Curriculum.

Possible Written/Spoken Outcomes or Incidental Writing/Speaking Opportunities

- Facts about Knuffle Bunny
- Lost poster for Knuffle Bunny
- Notices for role play area
- Instructions for using washing machine
- Baby talk dictionary
- Speech bubbles for Trixie where she is using baby talk - what she could be saying
- Write some advice for Trixie on keeping Knuffle Bunny safe
- Write story or part of story
- Make concertina book using black and white photographs and cartoon figures to create story
- Add captions or sentences as appropriate
- Draw own special toy. Write why it is special.

EYFS

Hook

- Set up role play area as a launderette with clothes and cloth toys
- Range of soft toys in different place inside and outside

1. Responding to the Text

- Book talk: Prediction - Look at illustration of Trixie crying. Who do you think she is? Why do you think she is upset?
- Book talk: Prediction - Look at the front cover. What do you think the story could be about? Have you any other ideas about why Trixie was upset now?
- Book talk: can you notice anything in the pictures and story that is unfamiliar? Where do you think this story is set?
- Book talk: Why do you think Mum knows what has happened to Knuffle Bunny?
- Book talk: Which part of the book do you like best? Can you say why?
- Book talk: Have you got any questions you would like to ask Trixie or her Dad or Mum?
- Book talk: Why do you think Trixie's mum and dad have a picture of her with Knuffle Bunny after she has found it?
- Writer talk: What do you think a Cautionary tale is?
- Book talk: Do you know any other stories about lost toys?
- Writer talk: Can you find any words that we don't use in our country? Can you find out what they mean?

2. Capturing Ideas

- Role play area set up as the Laundromat
- Small world play set up with locations in book
- Story map of Knuffle Bunny
- Retell story with focus on correct use of prepositions
- Look at pictures of Trixie's face. Generate/match feelings words.
- Think of times when they have felt the same emotions.
- Take photos to create new journey
- Use photos as prompts to make new story map for different story
- Retell new story with focus on use of prepositions
- Create route outside that children can follow with labels/instructions (Go past the bike shed, go through the tunnel, go under the slide etc)
- Bring in own special toy and say why it is special
- Invite parents/grandparents/carers to talk about a special toy they used to have

Sentence Games (use throughout unit)

- Sentence not a sentence game based on book
- Chain writing with a focus on creating accurate sentence with noun, adjective and verb
- Prepositions game based on book
- Hide a toy/Knuffle Bunny. Ask questions using prepositions to guess where it is.

Guided Reading Possibilities

- Explore Knuffle Bunny in detail - opportunities to look at illustrations as well as responding to and discussing book.
- Other books by Mo Willems
- Other stories about favourite/lost toys - Where's my Teddy? by Jez Alborough, Dogger by Shirley Hughes, I Love You, Blue Kangaroo by Emma Chichester Clark

Spoken Language

- Responding to questions in full sentences - responses should be clearly modelled. For example - My favourite toy is...because...
- Use structure to explain feelings - I felt...when..., When I was little I... Now I am big I can...
- Learn story and perform
- Thinking of questions to ask Trixie, Mum or Dad

Modelled Writing
Shared Writing
Guided Writing
Independent Writing

MAKING LINKS ACROSS THE CURRICULUM

Knowledge and Understanding of the World
- Understanding about growth and what you can do now compared with what you could do when you were little.
- Find USA and New York on the globe/map
- How a washing machine works. If there is a machine in school, use it to wash role play clothes, doll clothes etc
- Use water tray to wash plastic items
- Play with bubbles in water tray, blow bubbles

Maths
- Using positional language (prepositions)
- 2-D/3-D shape names to construct buildings for story

ICT
- Have video of story available for children to access
- Take photos in black and white around school or local area
- Beebot journeys

PSED
- Managing feelings
- Making links with own experiences when they have lost a favourite toy

Useful links
http://www.mowillems.com/
https://www.youtube.com/watch?v=CFksmnUUUDg

Creative Development
- Draw cartoon figures to put on black and white photos taken in locations around school or locally
- Large cardboard boxes to make washing machines
- Make models of buildings for small world play or outside chalked story map
- Bubble paintings with soapy water

Year R: What do I know about me?

The Learning Challenge CURRICULUM

Author: Mo Willems
Publisher: Walker Books
ISBN- 13:978-1844280599

Planning for Quality Texts EYFS: Oi! Get off our Train

These documents are intended to support the planning of effective literacy units based on high quality books. They are not intended to be lesson plans, but offer a menu of possible ideas for teachers to use as starting points to plan for purposeful learning and give pupils reasons for writing as well as the skills they need to write with impact on their reader. They follow a learning sequence:

- a hook to fully engage and interest the children
- responding to reading activities to allow immersion in and exploration of the text, including picture exploration, book and writer talk
- capturing ideas activities which include drama and talk to support understanding of the text and to develop vocabulary, language and ideas for writing
- activities focused on the development of spoken language and vocabulary development
- sentence games to develop creativity and the understanding of the concept of a sentence
- links to guided reading
- a range of writing tasks which may be guided in a focus group or incidental opportunities both in and outside the classroom

Specific mention is made of the writing sequence:

- modelled writing - teacher models the writing process aloud and the decisions writers make about sentences and word choices to create impact on the reader. This can also include the modelling of oral rehearsal of sentences and application of phonic learning.
- shared writing - collaborative composition with discussion and suggestions about what to write and how to write it to create the intended effect. At this point children may write a sentence/s, often in pairs, on whiteboards which are then discussed.
- guided writing - small group sessions based on specific needs of a specific group of children. The session may address misconceptions, bridge gaps or extend learning and can take place at any point during the unit.

In addition, cross-curricular links are suggested, including links to challenges from the Learning Challenge Curriculum.

Possible Written/Spoken Outcomes or Incidental Writing/Speaking Opportunities

- Train ticket
- Passenger checklist
- Weather chart
- Sun, raindrop, snowflake shaped books or paper to record activities done in this sort of weather
- List of animals on train
- Story map
- List of other endangered animals
- Picture of endangered animal with caption
- Picture of endangered animal with reason for wanting to get on train
- Speech bubble for animal asking to get on the train
- Who am I? lift the flap or locking book with clue about picture of animal inside
- Train shaped paper to write new version of The Wheels on the Train

EYFS

Hook

- Set up train set in room
- Visit to ride on a steam train
- Visit to zoo

1. Responding to the Text

- Book talk: Before reading - Have you ever been on a train? What was it like? Where did you go?
- Book talk: Who is the train driver?
- Book talk: Why does the driver let the elephant get on the train?
- Book talk: Why does the driver let the seal get on the train?
- Book talk: Why does the driver let the crane on the train?
- Book talk: Why does the driver let the tiger get on the train?
- Book talk: Why does the driver let the polar bear on the train?
- Book talk: Which part of the book do you like best? Can you say why?
- Book talk: Do you think the writer is trying to teach us something in the story? What do you think it is?
- Book talk: Do you think the boy was dreaming??

2. Capturing Ideas

- Life-size train set up inside and outside for retelling story
- Train set with small world animals to retell story
- Mini-environments for each habitat in story - sea, marsh, forest, Frozen North
- Story map - use train tracks
- Retell story using repetitive language from book
- Explore the meanings of the unfamiliar words - shovel, muck about, marsh etc.
- Look at all the weather types in the book. Look at what the characters do in the weather. Explore other things that can be done in the different weathers.
- Find out about other animals that are endangered and what is happening to their habitats
- Draw another endangered animal that might want to get on the train
- Devising clues for Who am I? game
- Use The Wheels on the Bus and change to The Wheels on the Train to develop new verses - The tigers on the train go roar, roar, roar

Sentence Games (use throughout unit)

- Sentence not a sentence game based on book
- Chain writing with a focus on creating accurate sentence with noun, adjective and verb
- Sound sort/Detective linked to current phonic learning

Guided Reading Possibilities

- Explore Oi! Get off our Train in detail - opportunities to look at illustrations as well as responding to and discussing book.
- Non-fiction books about endangered animals
- Non-fiction books about trains

Spoken Language

- Responding to questions in full sentences - responses should be clearly modelled. For example - The elephant got on the train because…, Please let me on your train because…, When it is sunny and hot, you can…
- Who am I? game - I have…, I am…, I live … Who am I? You are a…
- Listen to and join in with poems and rhymes about trains - Early in the morning, down by the station, The song of the Train

Modelled Writing
Shared Writing
Guided Writing
Independent Writing

MAKING LINKS ACROSS THE CURRICULUM

Knowledge and Understanding of the World

- Different types of weather
- Clothes and activities linked to each weather type
- Keep a weather chart
- Animals and where they live
- Endangered animals and reasons why they are endangered

Maths

- Days of the week for weather chart
- Devising symbols for weather types
- Use different triangles to form kite shape
- Buying and selling train tickets

ICT

- Have video of story available for children to access
- Look for information and pictures about endangered animals

PSED

- Looking after our world and the creatures in it
- Making links with own experiences

Useful links

http://vimeo.com/5643527

Creative Development

- Animal masks
- Large cardboard boxes to create trains
- Make life-size animals
- Make kites

Nursery: How do I get about?

Year R: Is everyone's home the same?

The Learning Challenge CURRICULUM

Author: John Burningham
Publisher: Red Fox
ISBN- 13:978-099853404

Planning for Quality Texts EYFS: Penguin

These documents are intended to support the planning of effective literacy units based on high quality books. They are not intended to be lesson plans, but offer a menu of possible ideas for teachers to use as starting points to plan for purposeful learning and give pupils reasons for writing as well as the skills they need to write with impact on their reader. They follow a learning sequence:

- a hook to fully engage and interest the children
- responding to reading activities to allow immersion in and exploration of the text, including picture exploration, book and writer talk
- capturing ideas activities which include drama and talk to support understanding of the text and to develop vocabulary, language and ideas for writing
- activities focused on the development of spoken language and vocabulary development
- sentence games to develop creativity and the understanding of the concept of a sentence
- links to guided reading
- a range of writing tasks which may be guided in a focus group or incidental opportunities both in and outside the classroom

Specific mention is made of the writing sequence:

- modelled writing - teacher models the writing process aloud and the decisions writers make about sentences and word choices to create impact on the reader. This can also include the modelling of oral rehearsal of sentences and application of phonic learning.
- shared writing - collaborative composition with discussion and suggestions about what to write and how to write it to create the intended effect. At this point children may write a sentence/s, often in pairs, on whiteboards which are then discussed.
- guided writing - small group sessions based on specific needs of a specific group of children. The session may address misconceptions, bridge gaps or extend learning and can take place at any point during the unit.

In addition, cross-curricular links are suggested, including links to challenges from the Learning Challenge Curriculum.

Possible Written/Spoken Outcomes or Incidental Writing/Speaking Opportunities

- Labelled picture of happy hat
- Thought bubbles for Penguin as Ben tries to make him laugh
- Speech bubbles for Penguin/record into Talking Tins or recordable speech bubbles
- List things that make you happy
- Make a concertina book of all the things Ben did to make Penguin laugh or talk
- Make a concertina book of other things Ben could try to make penguin laugh or talk
- Draw/write another adventure Ben could have with Penguin
- Present shaped paper in writing area
- Facts about penguins
- Recipe for a penguin snack
- Menu for a penguin café
- Price list for hat shop
- Labels for hats in hat shop

EYFS

Hook

- Large box wrapped as present in book
- Role play area set up as penguin café or hat shop

1. Responding to the Text

- Book talk: Prediction - Look at picture of gift. What do you think might be inside? Why do you think Ben is getting a present?
- Book talk: Why do you think Penguin does not laugh or talk to Ben?
- Book talk: Why did Ben try to feed Penguin to Lion?
- Book talk: Prediction - Look at the page where Lion has eaten Ben. What do you think is going to happen next?
- Book talk: Do you think the lion is frightening? Can you say why?
- Book talk: How can you tell that Ben is getting more and more angry?
- Book talk: Which part of the book do you like best? Can you say why?
- Book talk: Have you got any questions you would like to ask Penguin?
- Writer talk: Why do you think the writer used pictures instead of words when Penguin spoke?
- Writer talk: What do you notice about the words where Ben is trying to make Penguin laugh or talk? (Funniest face, happy hat etc)

2. Capturing Ideas

- Role play area set up as hat shop or a penguin cafe
- Role play what Penguin might have said to Ben
- Use Penguin's speech bubble as a story map to retell the story
- Use pictures of Ben and decide on words to describe how he is feeling
- Order pictures and words
- Make masks from paper plates for different emotions
- Find all the verbs that show what Ben does. Act them out.
- What would you like to find in a gift?
- Make a snack for a penguin
- Role play other things Ben could have done to make Penguin laugh or talk
- Other adventures that Ben could have with Penguin
- Play alliteration game with a bag of objects - name and add an alliteration

Sentence Games (use throughout unit)

- Sentence not a sentence game based on book
- Chain writing with a focus on creating accurate sentence with noun, adjective and verb
- Make other words from title - Penguin - applying phonics

Guided Reading Possibilities

- Explore Penguin in detail - opportunities to look at illustrations as well as responding to and discussing book.
- Non-fiction books about penguins
- Rhymes - Twinkle, Twinkle Little Star/Hey Diddle, Diddle

Spoken Language

- Responding to questions in full sentences - responses should be clearly modelled. For example - Ben felt...when Penguin...
- Sentence structure - Ben could...with Penguin.
- Develop vocabulary with emotion words and verbs
- Learn story and perform
- Think of questions to ask Penguin

Modelled Writing
Shared Writing
Guided Writing
Independent Writing

MAKING LINKS ACROSS THE CURRICULUM

Knowledge and Understanding of the World	Maths	ICT
• Penguins' habitat - cold places • Find North Pole on the globe • Investigating freezing and melting - ice blocks in water tray	• 3-D shapes • Ordering parcels by size - comparative language • Handling coins in hat shop/penguin cafe	• Have video of story available for children to access • Look for information and pictures of the North Pole and Penguins
PSED • What makes you laugh? • How can you show someone that you care and make them happy? • Describing feelings		**Useful links** https://vimeo.com/58744168 https://www.youtube.com/watch?v=L7tWNwhSocE
Creative Development • Make penguin puppets • Design and make own happy hat • Design other hats for hat shop • Create name in the style of the title, using a range of materials	The Learning Challenge CURRICULUM	
Author: Polly Dunbar **Publisher: Walker Books** **ISBN- 13:978-1-4063-1246-1**		

Planning for Quality Texts EYFS: The Acorn

These documents are intended to support the planning of effective literacy units based on high quality books. They are not intended to be lesson plans, but offer a menu of possible ideas for teachers to use as starting points to plan for purposeful learning and give pupils reasons for writing as well as the skills they need to write with impact on their reader. They follow a learning sequence:

- a hook to fully engage and interest the children
- responding to reading activities to allow immersion in and exploration of the text, including picture exploration, book and writer talk
- capturing ideas activities which include drama and talk to support understanding of the text and to develop vocabulary, language and ideas for writing
- activities focused on the development of spoken language and vocabulary development
- sentence games to develop creativity and the understanding of the concept of a sentence
- links to guided reading
- a range of writing tasks which may be guided in a focus group or incidental opportunities both in and outside the classroom

Specific mention is made of the writing sequence:

- modelled writing - teacher models the writing process aloud and the decisions writers make about sentences and word choices to create impact on the reader. This can also include the modelling of oral rehearsal of sentences and application of phonic learning.
- shared writing - collaborative composition with discussion and suggestions about what to write and how to write it to create the intended effect. At this point children may write a sentence/s, often in pairs, on whiteboards which are then discussed.
- guided writing - small group sessions based on specific needs of a specific group of children. The session may address misconceptions, bridge gaps or extend learning and can take place at any point during the unit.

In addition, cross-curricular links are suggested, including links to challenges from the Learning Challenge Curriculum.

Possible Written/Spoken Outcomes or Incidental Writing/Speaking Opportunities

- Label tree
- Draw life cycle of acorn/seed growing into tree and recount orally
- Seed/bean diary
- Story map with some key sentences
- Speech bubbles for other reasons acorn gave for not eating it
- Seed shaped paper in writing area
- Draw and label forest animal
- Drawing with title or caption or sentence for other forest animals
- New page for book with different animal using sentence model from book
- Sentences about other food the animals could eat, giving reasons

EYFS

Hook

- Go on an acorn/conker hunt
- Forest walk

1. Responding to the Text

- Book talk: Prediction - What might the story be about?
- Book talk: Prediction - after first page - Why do you think the acorn did not want the mouse to eat it?
- Book talk: What do you think the mouse could eat instead of the acorn? (This could be discussed for the other animals)
- Book talk: Which part of the book do you like best? Can you say why?
- Book talk: Look at the blurb. It says that the little acorn has ambition. What does ambition mean?
- Book talk: What do you think will happen to the acorn that rolled away at the end of the story?
- Book talk: Do you know any other stories about seeds growing?
- Book talk: Do you know any other stories where a character has to stop other characters from eating it?
- Writer talk: Can you find the sentences that are repeated?

2. Capturing Ideas

- Role play area set up as
- Make story map
- Retell story orally from story map with focus on the repetitive sentences
- Small world resources to retell or develop story
- What else might the acorn have said to the creatures to stop them from eating it? Role play conversations
- What else could they have eaten? Complete a grid with ideas.
- Grow bean or other seeds
- Guess the sounds and name forest animals from video(see link on next page)
- Find out about other forest animals that might have eaten the acorn.
- How would they have moved off? Find movement verbs and act them?
- Role play the conversation between the new animal and the acorn.

Sentence Games (use throughout unit)

- Sentence not a sentence game based on book
- Chain writing with a focus on creating accurate sentence with noun, adjective and verb
- Movement verbs

Guided Reading Possibilities

- Explore The Acorn in detail - opportunities to look at illustrations as well as responding to and discussing book.
- Apply phonic knowledge to read text
- Read other stories about growth - Little Acorn Grows Up - Edward Gibbs, Jasper's Beanstalk - Mick Inkpen, The Tiny Seed - Eric Carle etc.

Spoken Language

- Responding to questions in full sentences - responses should be clearly modelled. For example - I think the acorn that rolled away will............ I like the...best because...
- Role play of conversations using book language
- Learn story and perform - focus on repetitive language
- Sentence to give alternative food suggestion for animal - The grey rabbit could eat grass because they have good teeth for nibbling.

Modelled Writing
Shared Writing
Guided Writing
Independent Writing

MAKING LINKS ACROSS THE CURRICULUM

Knowledge and Understanding of the World
- Forest animals and what they like to eat
- Different forest trees and their seeds
- What seeds need to grow

PSED
- Allowing seeds to grow and looking after the environment

Maths
- Counting and number recognition with acorns, conkers etc
- Comparative sizes of animals

ICT
- Research forest animals
- Research forest trees

Useful links
https://www.youtube.com/watch?v=ZK4LjURtaDw
http://www.bbc.co.uk/programmes/p007l35f
https://www.youtube.com/watch?v=f3YTvT3gqFI

Creative Development
- Make animal masks
- Close observational drawing of seeds
- Make flap book with forest creatures

Year N: What happened to Jack's beans?

The Learning Challenge
CURRICULUM

Author: Edward Gibbs
Publisher: Brubaker, Ford and Friends
ISBN- 978099408390

Planning for Quality Texts EYFS: The Tiger who Came to Tea

These documents are intended to support the planning of effective literacy units based on high quality books. They are not intended to be lesson plans, but offer a menu of possible ideas for teachers to use as starting points to plan for purposeful learning and give pupils reasons for writing as well as the skills they need to write with impact on their reader. They follow a learning sequence:

- a hook to fully engage and interest the children
- responding to reading activities to allow immersion in and exploration of the text, including picture exploration, book and writer talk
- capturing ideas activities which include drama and talk to support understanding of the text and to develop vocabulary, language and ideas for writing
- activities focused on the development of spoken language and vocabulary development
- sentence games to develop creativity and the understanding of the concept of a sentence
- links to guided reading
- a range of writing tasks which may be guided in a focus group or incidental opportunities both in and outside the classroom

Specific mention is made of the writing sequence:

- modelled writing - teacher models the writing process aloud and the decisions writers make about sentences and word choices to create impact on the reader. This can also include the modelling of oral rehearsal of sentences and application of phonic learning.
- shared writing - collaborative composition with discussion and suggestions about what to write and how to write it to create the intended effect. At this point children may write a sentence/s, often in pairs, on whiteboards which are then discussed.
- guided writing - small group sessions based on specific needs of a specific group of children. The session may address misconceptions, bridge gaps or extend learning and can take place at any point during the unit.

In addition, cross-curricular links are suggested, including links to challenges from the Learning Challenge Curriculum.

Possible Written/Spoken Outcomes or Incidental Writing/Speaking Opportunities

- List of things the tiger ate and drank
- List of food for picnic on the moon
- Menu for tea party
- Menu for cafe
- Invitation to tea party
- Facts on tigers
- Animal shaped paper, paper plates in writing area
- Thought bubbles for different characters at different times in the story
- Make own story map Of The Tiger who Came to Tea
- Make story map of different animal who came to tea
- Lines for new rhyme based on Jelly on a Plate

EYFS

Hook

- Table set up for tea
- Kitchen scene from book after the tiger has left re-created

1. Responding to the Text

- Book talk: Prediction - Who do you think is ringing the doorbell?
- Book talk: Do you think your mummy would have asked the Tiger to come in for tea? Can you say why?
- Book talk: Do you think the Tiger was polite?
- Book talk: Where do you think the Tiger came from?
- Book talk: What do you think daddy thought when Sophie and her mummy told him what had happened?
- Book talk: Which part of the book do you like best? Can you say why?
- Book talk: Have you got any questions you would like to ask Sophie or Sophie's mummy?
- Book talk: Do you think the Tiger will ever come to tea again?
- Book talk: What do you think might be in the Tiger food?
- Writer talk: Can you find the words that the writer uses to tell us what the Tiger looked like?

2. Capturing Ideas

- Role play area set up as Sophie's kitchen/cafe
- People who come to our doors
- Food and drink that could have been in Sophie's fridge
- Food and drink that the tiger liked best
- Hot seat the Tiger
- Favourite supper - make a plate
- Healthy foods - make a plate
- Places you like to go to eat
- Story map
- Retell story orally from picture sequence or story map
- Make a timeline of Sophie's day
- Make tea for a tiger/tiger food
- What other animal might come to tea? Think of three adjectives to tell us what the animal is like.
- What would they eat?
- Plan a Tiger tea party
- Use Jelly on a Plate to create new lines for other foods - ice cream in a cone, lollies on a stick, samosas in your hands, soup in a spoon etc
- Add sounds or movements to each line - drip, drop, steam, crunch etc

Sentence Games (use throughout unit)

- Sentence not a sentence game based on book
- Chain writing with a focus on creating accurate sentence with noun, adjective and verb
- Sound sort/Detective linked to current phonic learning

Guided Reading Possibilities

- Explore The Tiger who Came to Tea in detail - opportunities to look at illustrations as well as responding to and discussing book.
- Non-fiction books about tigers
- Non-fiction books about restaurants and food
- Tasty Poems by Jill Bennett, Rhyme - Jelly on a Plate

Spoken Language

- Responding to questions in full sentences - responses should be clearly modelled. For example - My favourite supper/food is...because..., I think a...might come to the door.
- Develop vocabulary for - naming and describing animals, naming and describing foods, verbs for poem
- Learn a Tasty Poem and perform
- Thinking of questions to ask the Tiger, Sophie and her mummy

Modelled Writing
Shared Writing
Guided Writing
Independent Writing

MAKING LINKS ACROSS THE CURRICULUM

Knowledge and Understanding of the World
- What tigers eat and where they live
- Cooking and preparing food for tea party
- Healthy foods
-

Maths
- Shopping to replace what the tiger ate and drank
- Ordering numbers on front doors
- Weighing/balancing ingredients for cooking

ICT
- Have video of story available for children to access
- Look for information and pictures of the moon and planets

PSED
- Does the tiger have good manners? How is it polite to behave if you are in someone else's house?
- Making links with own experiences

Useful links
https://www.youtube.com/watch?v=BUOEGwCdYaE
https://www.youtube.com/watch?v=HqifY7ium4Q
https://www.youtube.com/watch?v=t_Re1dToPZM

Creative Development
- Making salt-dough food
- Look at Rousseau painting - Tiger in a Tropical Storm. Patterns of tiger's coat. Camouflage.
- Tiger masks
- Design a label for a tin or box of Tiger Food

Year N: Who are the famous animals in my books?

Year R: Who are the famous characters in my books?

The Learning Challenge
CURRICULUM

Author: Judith Kerr
Publisher: Harper Collins Children's Books
ISBN- 13:978- 0007215997

Planning for Quality Texts EYFS: Whatever Next!

These documents are intended to support the planning of effective literacy units based on high quality books. They are not intended to be lesson plans, but offer a menu of possible ideas for teachers to use as starting points to plan for purposeful learning and give pupils reasons for writing as well as the skills they need to write with impact on their reader. They follow a learning sequence:

- a hook to fully engage and interest the children
- responding to reading activities to allow immersion in and exploration of the text, including picture exploration, book and writer talk
- capturing ideas activities which include drama and talk to support understanding of the text and to develop vocabulary, language and ideas for writing
- activities focused on the development of spoken language and vocabulary development
- sentence games to develop creativity and the understanding of the concept of a sentence
- links to guided reading
- a range of writing tasks which may be guided in a focus group or incidental opportunities both in and outside the classroom

Specific mention is made of the writing sequence:

- modelled writing - teacher models the writing process aloud and the decisions writers make about sentences and word choices to create impact on the reader. This can also include the modelling of oral rehearsal of sentences and application of phonic learning.
- shared writing - collaborative composition with discussion and suggestions about what to write and how to write it to create the intended effect. At this point children may write a sentence/s, often in pairs, on whiteboards which are then discussed.
- guided writing - small group sessions based on specific needs of a specific group of children. The session may address misconceptions, bridge gaps or extend learning and can take place at any point during the unit.

In addition, cross-curricular links are suggested, including links to challenges from the Learning Challenge Curriculum.

Possible Written/Spoken Outcomes or Incidental Writing/Speaking Opportunities • List of things needed for journey • List of food for picnic on the moon • Menu for moon picnic • Speech bubbles for Owl and Baby Bear • Question for Baby Bear • Moon and star shaped paper for writing about what Baby Bear saw • Clipboards for spaceship pre take-off checklist • Label picture/diagram of rocket/spaceship • Story map of text • Story map of own journey • Zig zag book for own space journey • Draw and label astronaut's clothes	**EYFS**  **Hook** • Set up role play area as the moon for children to discover •	**1. Responding to the Text** • Book talk: Prediction - Where do you think Baby Bear is going? • Book talk: How do you think Baby Bear was feeling as he whizzed through the sky? • Book talk: Do you think Mrs. Bear believes him? • Book talk: Does Baby Bear really go to the moon? Do you think he is brave? • Book talk: Which part of the book do you like best? Can you say why? • Book talk: Have you got any questions you would like to ask Baby Bear? • Writer talk: Mrs. Bear says "Look at the *state* of you!" What do you think she means? • Book talk: Do you know any other stories about going to the moon? • Writer talk: What do you notice about how some of the sentences are written on the pages?
2. Capturing Ideas • Role play area set up as the moon • Moonscape obstacle course • Stick puppets to retell story • Role play conversation between Owl and Baby Bear • Hot seat Baby Bear • Make picture sequence or story map • Retell story orally from picture sequence or story map • Checks on spaceship before take-off • What would you wear to the moon? Different resources available • Plan a moon picnic • Make items for moon picnic • Moonscapes in sand tray • What might Baby Bear have seen on the moon? • Mum says "Whatever next?" What other adventure might Baby Bear have? • What would you see on your space journey?	**Sentence Games (use throughout unit)** • Sentence not a sentence game based on book • Chain writing with a focus on creating accurate sentence with noun, adjective and verb • Sound sort/Detective linked to current phonic learning **Guided Reading Possibilities** • Explore Whatever Next! in detail - opportunities to look at illustrations as well as responding to and discussing book. • Non-fiction books about space • Rhymes - Twinkle, Twinkle Little Star/Hey Diddle, Diddle	**Spoken Language** • Responding to questions in full sentences - responses should be clearly modelled. For example - On my space journey I saw... • Baby Bear goes "whoosh" as he flies through the air. Collect more words that we use for moving fast and slowly • Learn story and perform • Thinking of questions to ask Baby Bear about his journey **Modelled Writing** **Shared Writing** **Guided Writing** **Independent Writing**

MAKING LINKS ACROSS THE CURRICULUM

Knowledge and Understanding of the World
- Mapping journey to the moon
- Make moonscapes on card bases
- Use coloured glitter as space/moon dust. Evaluate different hats, including the colander as protection.
- Make a spinning planet - card circle with sparkly decorations with pencil in centre to make spinner

Maths
- Counting down from 10
- Ordering numbers
- Make stars with triangles

ICT
- Have video of story available for children to access
- Look for information and pictures of the moon and planets

PSED
- Differences - aliens and humans. But, Martin! text by June Counsell
- Making links with own experiences

Useful links
http://vimeo.com/75139220

Creative Development
- Model making - aliens/moon houses, space ships
- Large cardboard boxes to create life-size space-ships
- Alien masks
- Pop-up Baby Bear coming out of chimney

Year R: Twinkle, twinkle little star. How I wonder what you are?

The Learning Challenge CURRICULUM

Author: Jill Murphy
Publisher: Macmillan Children's Books
ISBN- 13:978-0230015470

Planning for Quality Texts EYFS: Where the Wild Things Are

These documents are intended to support the planning of effective literacy units based on high quality books. They are not intended to be lesson plans, but offer a menu of possible ideas for teachers to use as starting points to plan for purposeful learning and give pupils reasons for writing as well as the skills they need to write with impact on their reader. They follow a learning sequence:

- a hook to fully engage and interest the children
- responding to reading activities to allow immersion in and exploration of the text, including picture exploration, book and writer talk
- capturing ideas activities which include drama and talk to support understanding of the text and to develop vocabulary, language and ideas for writing
- activities focused on the development of spoken language and vocabulary development
- sentence games to develop creativity and the understanding of the concept of a sentence
- links to guided reading
- a range of writing tasks which may be guided in a focus group or incidental opportunities both in and outside the classroom

Specific mention is made of the writing sequence:

- modelled writing - teacher models the writing process aloud and the decisions writers make about sentences and word choices to create impact on the reader. This can also include the modelling of oral rehearsal of sentences and application of phonic learning.
- shared writing - collaborative composition with discussion and suggestions about what to write and how to write it to create the intended effect. At this point children may write a sentence/s, often in pairs, on whiteboards which are then discussed.
- guided writing - small group sessions based on specific needs of a specific group of children. The session may address misconceptions, bridge gaps or extend learning and can take place at any point during the unit.

In addition, cross-curricular links are suggested, including links to challenges from the Learning Challenge Curriculum.

Possible Written/Spoken Outcomes or Incidental Writing/Speaking Opportunities

- Label a picture of a Wild Thing
- Label own Wild Thing
- Story map with some key sentences
- Message in a bottle back to Max
- Lost poster for a Wild Thing
- Question for Max
- Island maps labelled with features
- Captions for pages without text
- Wild Thing and boat shaped paper
- Thought bubbles for characters
- Speech bubbles for characters
- Apology note from max to his mother
- Menu for wild rumpus

EYFS

WHERE THE WILD THINGS ARE

STORY AND PICTURES BY MAURICE SENDAK

Hook

- Message in a bottle from Max
- Max's boat in classroom

1. Responding to the Text

- Book talk: Prediction - What might the story be about?
- Book talk: What does mischief mean?
- Book talk: What mischief did Max make?
- Book talk: Do you ever make mischief? What kind of mischief do you make?
- Book talk: Which part of the book do you like best? Can you say why?
- Book talk: Do you think the Wild Things are "terrible"?
- Book talk: How do you think the King felt when Max became King?
- Book talk: How do you think the Wild Things feel when Max leaves?
- Book talk: Why don't the Wild Things go with Max?
- Writer talk: Can you find some adjectives that tell us about the Wild Things?
- Writer talk: Can you say what happens in the beginning, in the middle and at the end of the story?

2. Capturing Ideas

- Role play area set up as Max's room. Could a jungle grow here? Make vines etc. to transform room.
- Stick puppets to retell story
- Make props for the story - crown, wolf ears, monster masks
- In role as Wild Things - how do they move?
- Role play the wild rumpus
- Make story map
- Retell story orally from story map
- Small world island to retell or develop story
- Chalked island in outdoor area. Chalks available for drawing own or adding features
- Explore how characters felt at different points in the story. What were they thinking? What were they saying?
- Watch sections from Monsters Inc and compare and discuss. Can monsters be friendly?
- Draw own Wild Thing
- Plan a wild rumpus - activities and food

Sentence Games (use throughout unit)

- Sentence not a sentence game based on book
- Chain writing with a focus on creating accurate sentence with noun, adjective and verb
- Adjectives that have talent to tell the reader more about the Wild Things - pointed teeth, green tongue etc.

Guided Reading Possibilities

- Explore Where the Wild Things Are in detail - opportunities to look at illustrations as well as responding to and discussing book.
- Apply phonic knowledge to read text
- Read other stories about monsters and compare them?

Spoken Language

- Responding to questions in full sentences - responses should be clearly modelled. For example - I make mischief when..., I am sorry because...
- Oral rehearsal of captions for illustrations without text
- Learn story and perform
- Thinking of questions to ask Max about his journey

Modelled Writing
Shared Writing
Guided Writing
Independent Writing

MAKING LINKS ACROSS THE CURRICULUM

Knowledge and Understanding of the World
- Habitats - habitat for Wild Things. Habitats for us.
- Naming landscape features - beach, lake, forest, mountains etc.
- Explore sinking and floating in water tray with different objects - types of water craft, containers for messages
- What is an island? Link with UK
- Other forms of transport Max could have used

Maths
- Times during the day - lunch-time, supper-time etc.
- Days of the week and today, tomorrow, yesterday

ICT
- Have video of story available for children to access

PSED
- Thinking about behaviour and consequences
- Making links with own experiences

Useful links
http://vimeo.com/75139220
https://www.youtube.com/watch?v=6cOEFnppm_A

Creative Development
- Leaf shapes and patterns from book to make designs/pictures
- Large cardboard boxes to create boat to sail away in
- Make Max's crown
- Make wolf ears

Year R: Who are the famous characters in my book?

The Learning Challenge CURRICULUM

Author: Maurice Sendak
Publisher: Red Fox
ISBN- 978099408390

KS1 MENUS

KEY STAGE 1 MENUS

Planning with Quality Texts: Aaaarrgghh! Spider!

These documents are intended to support the planning of effective literacy units based on high quality picture books. They are not intended to be lesson plans, but offer a menu of possible ideas for teachers to use as starting points to plan for purposeful learning and give pupils reasons for writing as well as the skills they need to write with impact on their reader. They follow a learning sequence:

- a hook to fully engage and interest the children
- responding to reading activities to allow immersion in and exploration of the text, including picture exploration, book and writer talk
- capturing ideas activities which include drama and talk to support understanding of the text and to develop vocabulary, language and ideas for writing
- possibilities for the contextualised teaching of grammar
- sentence games to develop creativity, vocabulary, language and grammar
- links to guided reading
- a range of writing tasks which may be final unit outcomes or incidental opportunities during the unit

Specific mention is made of the writing sequence:

- modelled writing - teacher models the writing process aloud and the decisions writers make about sentences, paragraphs etc to create impact on the reader. This can also include the modelling of planning and spelling strategies.
- shared writing - collaborative composition with discussion and suggestions about what to write and how to write it to create the intended effect. At this point children may write a sentence/s, often in pairs, on whiteboards which are then discussed.
- guided writing - small group sessions based on specific needs of a specific group of children. The session may address misconceptions, bridge gaps or extend learning and can take place at any point during the unit.

In addition, cross-curricular links are suggested, including links to challenges from the Learning Challenge Curriculum.

Possible Written Outcomes or Incidental Writing Opportunities

- Sentences based on model in text - Look at me! I can...
- Thought bubbles
- Retelling of story oral or written, as appropriate
- Labelling spider or other mini-beast or creature
- Captions as above
- Fact box on spider or other creatures
- Write story with another creature wanting to be a family pet
- Spider poems
- What I would like to have as a pet
- Instructions - how to look after a ...

RECEPTION AND YEAR 1

Hook

- Pets visiting school with owners
- Visit from "zoo man" or to a zoo
- Go on a web or spider hunt
- Turn role play area/book corner into a web

1. Responding to the Text

- Use front cover to predict what might be happening
- Read up to page with the spider invasion and predict what they think may happen
- **Book talk:** What did you like about the story? Was there anything you did not like?
- **Book talk:** Does the story remind you of anything? Does it make you think of any questions?
- Join in with repeated phrases in the book
- Look at the double page of the silver spider webs. How does it make you feel? Can you think of any adjectives? What does it remind you of?
- Read other spider stories and rhymes

2. Capturing Ideas

- What might the world look like from a spider's point of view? Draw classroom or other room from spider's point of view
- Think of questions and hot seat spider and/or family members
- Think about why people are afraid of spiders?
- What other creatures might people be afraid of Why?
- Gather facts about spiders for display
- Story map - annotate with key language. Use for oral retelling
- Create story map for story with different creature - annotate with key language. Use for oral retelling
- Role play story using puppets, small world resources etc
- Choosing an animal the y would like as a pet and saying why. Sentence structure identified - I would like a ... because ...

Sentence Games (use throughout unit)

- Sentence not a sentence game
- Human sentences
- Action verb game - children act out movement verbs and rehearse sentences
- Chain writing with spiders/webs as starting point, using features appropriate to year group
- Conjunction game with identified conjunctions as appropriate

Guided Reading Possibilities

- Look at non-fiction texts about spiders and other mini-beasts
- Read other books about mini-beasts - The Very Hungry Caterpillar and others by Eric Carle, The Snail and The Whale by Julia Donaldson and the Anansi stories
- Identify and discuss features of text type for final written outcome. Level of text can be pitched at each groups' level, ensuring both access and challenge.

3. Contextualised Grammar Teaching

- Concept of a sentence
- Joining extending sentences with identified conjunctions as appropriate
- Using well-chosen verbs and adjectives to describe spiders/webs/movement

4. Modelled Writing
Shared Writing
Guided Writing
Independent Writing

MAKING LINKS ACROSS THE CURRICULUM

Science
- Spider/mini-beast habitats

Art
- Creating web designs with silver pens, paint, glitter, wool, string
- Thumbprint spiders

Maths
- Counting spiders and their legs
- Ordering spiders by size

Dance
- Spider/mini-beast movements
- Mini-beast dance

KS1 Science:
Why humans are not like tigers?

The Learning Challenge CURRICULUM

Author: Lydia Monks
Publisher: Egmont Books
ISBN: 978-1405223195

Planning for Quality Texts: Naughty Bus

These documents are intended to support the planning of effective literacy units based on high quality books. They are not intended to be lesson plans, but offer a menu of possible ideas for teachers to use as starting points to plan for purposeful learning and give pupils reasons for writing as well as the skills they need to write with impact on their reader. They follow a learning sequence:

- a hook to fully engage and interest the children
- responding to reading activities to allow immersion in and exploration of the text, including picture exploration, book and writer talk
- capturing ideas activities which include drama and talk to support understanding of the text and to develop vocabulary, language and ideas for writing
- possibilities for the contextualised teaching of grammar
- sentence games to develop creativity, vocabulary, language and grammar
- links to guided reading
- a range of writing tasks which may be final unit outcomes or incidental opportunities during the unit

Specific mention is made of the writing sequence:

- modelled writing - teacher models the writing process aloud and the decisions writers make about sentences, paragraphs etc to create impact on the reader. This can also include the modelling of planning and spelling strategies.
- shared writing - collaborative composition with discussion and suggestions about what to write and how to write it to create the intended effect. At this point children may write a sentence/s, often in pairs, on whiteboards which are then discussed.
- guided writing - small group sessions based on specific needs of a specific group of children. The session may address misconceptions, bridge gaps or extend learning and can take place at any point during the unit.

In addition, cross-curricular links are suggested, including links to challenges from the Learning Challenge Curriculum.

RECEPTION AND YEAR 1

Possible Written Outcomes or Incidental Writing Opportunities

- Thank you letter
- Retell of story or one event
- Recount of bus ride or visit
- Bus tickets
- Bus pass
- Speech bubbles for characters at the bus stop before and after the bus goes past
- Add new event for the bus that takes place at night
- Photo story of bus adventure round the school - labels, captions, text as appropriate
- Instructions - How to catch a naughty bus
- Non -fiction writing on other types of transport - fact files
- Calligram class collection
- Poem based on The Wheels on the Bus

Hook

- Bus ride
- Visit to a bus station
- Children discover a wrapped gift containing a toy bus

1. Responding to the Text

- Visual literacy: What kind of pictures are there in the book? Do you know any other books like this? Do you like the pictures in the book?
- Book talk: Who is talking in the book? How do we know?
- Book talk: Do you think it is the bus that is being naughty?
- Book talk: Why do we not see the boy properly until the end of the book?
- Book talk: Which part of the book do you like best? Can you say why?
- Book talk: Have you got any questions you would like to ask the naughty bus?
- Writer talk: Spot the different sentence types
- Writer talk: The writers have written some of the words and sentences in different ways. Can you find some of them?
- Writer talk: Can you choose one example and say why you think the writers have written the word or sentence differently? Do you think this helps us to understand the story better?

2. Capturing Ideas

- Role play area set up as bus
- Make a picture sequence or story map
- Retell story orally from picture sequence or story map
- Add time adverbs to the map and incorporate in retell
- Role play the characters at the bus stop before and after the bus goes past
- Find other places the naughty bus might go? What might happen?
- Think of places it might go to at night. What might happen?
- Use small world resources to create and role play a night time or additional event
- Take photos of new event and sequence
- Look at some other examples of calligrams and give children some words to create their own. For example - cold, messy, dangerous, skidded, speeded, crawled.
- Add calligram/s to the sequence of new event

Sentence Games (use throughout unit)

- Sentence not a sentence game
- Chain writing with a focus on strong verbs, correct tense formation
- Adjectives with talent game - choosing the best adjective for sentences about the bus
- Naming the noun using different types of transport

Guided Reading Possibilities

- Explore The Naughty Bus in detail - opportunities to look at calligrams, use of font and sentences as well as responding to and discussing book.
- Non-fiction books about buses and other forms of transport
- Identify and discuss features of text type for final written outcome. Level of text can be pitched at each groups' level, ensuring both access and challenge.

3. Contextualised Grammar Teaching

- Reinforce concept of a sentence
- Different sentence types - statement, question, exclamation
- Choice of verbs to describe the bus' movements
- Time adverbs to sequence events

4. Modelled Writing
Shared Writing
Guided Writing
Independent Writing

MAKING LINKS ACROSS THE CURRICULUM

Geography/Science/History
- Routes and maps - plan a new route for the naughty bus
- Give directions for bus to follow
- Investigate a local bus route - how else could you reach the destination
- Look at older buses and trams

Maths
- Counting people at the bus stop
- Cost of bus ticket - buying and selling tickets, giving change

ICT
- Create the naughty bus' route and use Beebot to follow it

PSHE

Useful links
http://www.youtube.com/watch?v=sqQ1BAEj1oE

Art/DT
- Create townscape for the naughty bus
- Paint backgrounds for the naughty bus' adventures
- Use different tyres to create prints and patterns

Year 1 Geography/History: Where did and do the wheels on the bus go?

The Learning Challenge CURRICULUM

Author: Jan and Jerry Oke
Publisher: Little Knowall Publishing
ISBN: 978-0-954-7921-1-4

Planning with Quality Texts: Bog Baby

These documents are intended to support the planning of effective literacy units based on high quality picture books. They are not intended to be lesson plans, but offer a menu of possible ideas for teachers to use as starting points to plan for purposeful learning and give pupils reasons for writing as well as the skills they need to write with impact on their reader. They follow a learning sequence:

- a hook to fully engage and interest the children
- responding to reading activities to allow immersion in and exploration of the text, including picture exploration, book and writer talk
- capturing ideas activities which include drama and talk to support understanding of the text and to develop vocabulary, language and ideas for writing
- possibilities for the contextualised teaching of grammar
- sentence games to develop creativity, vocabulary, language and grammar
- links to guided reading
- a range of writing tasks which may be final unit outcomes or incidental opportunities during the unit

Specific mention is made of the writing sequence:

- modelled writing - teacher models the writing process aloud and the decisions writers make about sentences, paragraphs etc to create impact on the reader. This can also include the modelling of planning and spelling strategies.
- shared writing - collaborative composition with discussion and suggestions about what to write and how to write it to create the intended effect. At this point children may write a sentence/s, often in pairs, on whiteboards which are then discussed.
- guided writing - small group sessions based on specific needs of a specific group of children. The session may address misconceptions, bridge gaps or extend learning and can take place at any point during the unit.

In addition, cross-curricular links are suggested, including links to challenges from the Learning Challenge Curriculum.

Possible Written Outcomes or Incidental Writing Opportunities	RECEPTION, YEAR 1 AND 2	1. Responding to the Text
• Message to a bog baby • List - what a bog baby needs • Instructions - how to look after a bog baby • Fact file/information form (included in text) • Letter to Jeanne Willis or Penguin Books to give further information not on form • Report on Bog babies - could be based on book or created bog baby. • Character profiles of different bog babies (use picture at the end of the book) • Invitation to a bog baby party • Party menu • Bog baby recipes • Bog baby story about visiting another environment • Create own creature and label/write captions/ write fact file/report. Possible class book The Bog Baby Spotters Guide.	 **Hook** • Go on a bog baby hunt • Letter/telephone message from bog baby professor asking for help to find out about bog babies • Visit to pond - pond dipping	• Use picture on front cover - What is this creature? Where might it live? What would we like to find out about it? • Picture exploration: look closely at the pictures of the pond and wood environment • Book talk: likes, dislikes, puzzles and reminders • Book talk: discuss why the girls kept the bog baby a secret , why mum was not cross when she found out and why the bog baby did not try to escape • Writer talk: look at the different size of the font, the use of print in bold, the font used for the first letter of the first word on some pages and how the word magic is printed • Writer talk: look at how the writer describes the bog baby - word choices, different sentence types - simple, compound and complex. Think about the effect.
2. Capturing Ideas • Role play area set up with objects from story/ stick puppets etc to enable retelling of story • Create alternative environments for the bog baby - develop vocabulary • Hot seat the 2 girls • Build word/sentence banks about the bog baby in the story • Build word/sentence banks for some of the other bog babies • Role play reporter interviewing bog baby spotter who has discovered a new bog baby • Plan a bog baby party - What would they play? What would they eat? • Draw calligrams for other words in text	**Sentence Games (use throughout unit)** • Sentence not a sentence game based on book • Fortunately game using picture prompts from Bog Baby text • Chain writing with bog babies as starting point, using features appropriate to year group • Conjunctions game - Bog babies live in ponds… **Guided Reading Possibilities** • Read ***The King of Tiny Things*** by Jeanne Willis and compare • Non-fiction texts on creatures and their environments • Identify and discuss features of text type for final written outcome. Level of text can be pitched at each groups' level, ensuring both access and challenge.	**3. Contextualised Grammar Teaching** • Nouns to name features of environment and bog babies. Extend to carefully chosen adjectives. • As applicable to year group, use features of environment and bog babies to look at using verbs and adverbs to add to description. • As applicable look at prepositions and use to support description of environment. (Next to the ferns, creamy flowers were growing. / On the waterlily pads were many different insects.) • Focus on concept of a sentence. • As applicable use of compound/complex sentences **4. Modelled Writing** **Shared Writing** **Guided Writing** **Independent Writing**

MAKING LINKS ACROSS THE CURRICULUM

Geography/Science

- Making a map showing bog babies' homes
- Explain why a bog baby cannot live like us
- Caring for living things

PSHE

- When should we keep secrets?
- Keeping creatures in their natural homes

Maths

- Measuring to build a shelter for a bog baby
- Weighing ingredients for bog baby food

Art/DT

- Make a bog baby (clay, sock puppet, finger puppet etc)
- Construct a shelter for a bog baby
- Painter study - Seurat and pointillism. Paint own bog baby habitats using technique

Useful links

- http://www.jeannewillis.com/BogText1.html

KS1 Science:
Why humans are not like tigers?

The Learning Challenge
CURRICULUM

Author: Jeanne Willis
Publisher: Schwartz and Wade Books
ISBN: 978-0375861765

Planning for Quality Texts: The Queen's Hat

These documents are intended to support the planning of effective literacy units based on high quality books. They are not intended to be lesson plans, but offer a menu of possible ideas for teachers to use as starting points to plan for purposeful learning and give pupils reasons for writing as well as the skills they need to write with impact on their reader. They follow a learning sequence:

- a hook to fully engage and interest the children
- responding to reading activities to allow immersion in and exploration of the text, including picture exploration, book and writer talk
- capturing ideas activities which include drama and talk to support understanding of the text and to develop vocabulary, language and ideas for writing
- possibilities for the contextualised teaching of grammar
- sentence games to develop creativity, vocabulary, language and grammar
- links to guided reading
- a range of writing tasks which may be final unit outcomes or incidental opportunities during the unit

Specific mention is made of the writing sequence:

- modelled writing - teacher models the writing process aloud and the decisions writers make about sentences, paragraphs etc. to create impact on the reader. This can also include the modelling of planning and spelling strategies.
- shared writing - collaborative composition with discussion and suggestions about what to write and how to write it to create the intended effect. At this point children may write a sentence/s, often in pairs, on whiteboards which are then discussed.
- guided writing - small group sessions based on specific needs of a specific group of children. The session may address misconceptions, bridge gaps or extend learning and can take place at any point during the unit.

In addition, cross-curricular links are suggested, including links to challenges from the Learning Challenge Curriculum.

RECEPTION, YEAR 1 AND 2

Possible Written Outcomes or Incidental Writing Opportunities

- Speech/thought bubbles for Queen, guardsmen or dog
- Oral retell of story
- Lost poster
- Journey of hat in zig-zag book
- Fact files on buildings in London
- Fact files on buildings in local town or city
- Plan a journey in nearest city or town
- Retell story in new location
- Retell story with different lost object
- Write in role as Queen or guardsman
- Design and label a new coat for the dog
- Design a new hat for the Queen
- Invitation to tea
- Tea party menu
- Tea party recipes
- Facts about guardsmen
- Write additional text for specific pages
- Write own version based on local town or city using language from book as a model

Hook

- Find hat in classroom or outside - lady's hat or guardsman's hat
- Letter from the Queen asking for help to find her hat
- Watch video of the changing of the guard

Responding to the Text

- Book talk: Use front cover. What might the book be about?
- Book talk: Look at the first page. Where do you think this building is? Who do you think might live there?
- Book talk: Why do you think the Queen has a dog with her? Why do you think it is wearing a patterned coat? What do you know about the pattern?
- Book talk: Where do you think the hat will land?
- Book talk: Where do you think the Queen is going?
- Book talk: Who do you think the Queen might be going to visit?
- Writer talk: How do you think the pictures help to tell the story?
- Writer talk: Can you find all the verbs that tell us how the hat moved?
- Writer talk: Why do you think the writer chose these words?
- Book talk: Do you like this story/ Why or why not?

2. Capturing Ideas

- Discuss each scene - What are the guardsmen doing? What is the Queen doing? What is the dog doing?
- Story map events and retell
- Freeze frame different events
- Develop questions for Queen/guardsman
- Hot seat Queen/guardsman
- Research landmark buildings from book
- Research local landmark buildings
- Word bank of movement verbs
- Develop story map for new journey in local city
- Annotate with language relevant to year group
- Retell new version in full sentences
- What else might the Queen have lost? Develop ideas.
- Plan a tea party - research food and recipes
- Learn and perform - Buckingham Palace by A.A. Milne
- Role play changing of the guard

Sentence Games (use throughout unit)

- Sentence not a sentence game
- Cline activity - movement verbs
- Zone of relevance - verbs
- Preposition game
- Sentence type game

Guided Reading Possibilities

- Katie in London - James Mayhew
- The Queen's Handbag - Steve Antony
- Non-fiction books on London or local city
- Rosie's Walk - Pat Hutchins
- Rosie's Chick - Pat Hutchins

3. Contextualised Grammar Teaching

- Reinforce concept of a sentence
- Verb choice - movement and pace
- Use or prepositions to express position
- Apostrophes for singular possession - the Queen's hat, the dog's coat etc.
- Questions, statements, exclamations and commands

4. Modelled Writing

Shared Writing

Guided Writing

Independent Writing

MAKING LINKS ACROSS THE CURRICULUM

Geography/Science/History
- Simple maps and routes
- City landmarks

Maths
- Counting, grouping guardsmen
- More than less than
- Doubling and halving

ICT
- Menu for tea party
- Researching landmarks

Music/PE
- Band music
- Marching to different rhythms
- Using instruments to create different rhythms

Useful links
http://www.dltk-kids.com/world/england/mmilne-buckinghampalace.htm
https://www.youtube.com/watch?v=fykC1P3J0eg
https://www.youtube.com/watch?v=pydofayMkxE
http://www.steveantony.com/the-queens-hat/

Art/DT
- Design a hat
- Line drawings of buildings in the style of the illustrator
- Patterns - tartans etc.
- Cooking - tea party food

Year 1 Geography/History: Where do and did the wheels on the bus go?
Year 2 Geography: What did ...find exciting about our town/city?
Year 2 Science: What materials did they use to build...?

The Learning Challenge CURRICULUM

Author: Steve Antony
Publisher: Hodder Children's Books
ISBN: 978-1-44491915-8

Planning for Quality Texts: The Rabbit Problem

These documents are intended to support the planning of effective literacy units based on high quality picture books. They are not intended to be lesson plans, but offer a menu of possible ideas for teachers to use as starting points to plan for purposeful learning and give pupils reasons for writing as well as the skills they need to write with impact on their reader. They follow a learning sequence:

- a hook to fully engage and interest the children
- responding to reading activities to allow immersion in and exploration of the text, including picture exploration, book and writer talk
- capturing ideas activities which include drama and talk to support understanding of the text and to develop vocabulary, language and ideas for writing
- possibilities for the contextualised teaching of grammar
- sentence games to develop creativity, vocabulary, language and grammar
- links to guided reading
- a range of writing tasks which may be final unit outcomes or incidental opportunities during the unit

Specific mention is made of the writing sequence:

- modelled writing - teacher models the writing process aloud and the decisions writers make about sentences, paragraphs etc to create impact on the reader. This can also include the modelling of planning and spelling strategies.
- shared writing - collaborative composition with discussion and suggestions about what to write and how to write it to create the intended effect. At this point children may write a sentence/s, often in pairs, on whiteboards which are then discussed.
- guided writing - small group sessions based on specific needs of a specific group of children. The session may address misconceptions, bridge gaps or extend learning and can take place at any point during the unit.

In addition, cross-curricular links are suggested, including links to challenges from the Learning Challenge Curriculum.

RECEPTION, YEAR 1 AND 2

Possible Written Outcomes or Incidental Writing Opportunities
- Postcard to a rabbit in another field
- Speech bubbles/thought bubbles at different points in the year
- Dialogue at different points in the year
- Advert for a "companion"
- Birth certificate for another rabbit
- Invitation to christening or a carrot feast
- Order forms
- Instructions - how to plant seeds/carrot recipes
- List - favourite rabbit names/foods liked or disliked
- Recommend a book for a bored rabbit to read
- Recount the sequence of events across the year
- A day in the life of…
- Invent another problem for the rabbits and create a calendar page
- Non-chronological report - The Fibonacci Rabbit
- Evaluate how well scarecrow worked

Hook
- Sign in classroom or outside - No… may leave…
- Scatter nibbled carrots and leave rabbit footprints. Children investigate what might have happened.

1. Responding to the Text
- Book talk: Use front cover - what might the problem be?
- Visual literacy: Explore the different calendar pages and discuss what is happening
- Book talk: what kind of book is this?
- Book talk: Have you any questions about it? Does it remind you of anything?
- Visual literacy: On July page, look at the rabbits' expressions on July and what they are doing. What can we find out?
- Book talk: Hot seat Lonely Rabbit or Chalk Rabbit at different points. Focus on how they feel during the year.
- Book talk: Where do you think the rabbits go at the end of the year? What do you think Lonely and Chalk do?
- Writer talk: Look at different pages in groups. What information do the calendar notes give us about the rabbits' lives?
- Writer talk: What do we know about what the rabbits need?

2. Capturing Ideas
- Set up small world play as Fibonacci's field
- Role play scenes from book, showing how the rabbits have different characters
- Sequence calendar pictures for working wall
- Following hot seating add feelings vocabulary to each picture.
- Use a cline to discuss the meaning and intensity of above vocabulary. Introduce more ambitious words and discuss.
- Annotate picture sequence display with time adverbials and generalising sentence openers
- Orally rehearse the sequence of events in sentences, using displayed pictures and language prompts
- Develop new problem for rabbits - how would they behave? How would the time of year or weather affect them? How would they solve the problem?
- Plan a dinner party for some Fibonacci rabbits

Sentence Games (use throughout unit)
- Sentence not a sentence game based on book
- Conjunctions game based on book
- Five disasters for a Fibonacci Rabbit
- Capture pictures in 2 adjectives/verb+adverb
- Add detail to a sentence - precise adjectives, strengthen verb, adverb/adverbial, relative clause

Guided Reading Possibilities
- Other Emily Gravett books - look at differences and similarities
- Other books about rabbits - Peter Rabbit and other Beatrix Potter stories, Brer Rabbit, The Velveteen Rabbit
- Identify and discuss features of text type for final written outcome. Level of text can be pitched at each groups' level, ensuring both access and challenge.

3. Contextualised Grammar Teaching
- Range of time adverbials, drawing on the time of the year, time of day (In Spring, When it rains, At night e.t.c).
- Linking words and phrases - generalising sentence starters (Many, Most, Usually, Some)
- Relative clauses to add detail – noun + who, whom, which or that

4. Modelled Writing
Shared Writing
Guided Writing
Independent Writing

MAKING LINKS ACROSS THE CURRICULUM

Geography/Science
- Weather/seasonal patterns
- Reading the temperature and recording
- Grow salad/vegetables

Maths
- Counting backwards and forwards to 100 and beyond
- Doubling
- Tallying
- Months of the year/seasons

DT/ICT
- Design and make a scarecrow
- Design and make a rabbit shelter
- Create new scene by drawing rabbits and adding to background picture - photograph. (See link below)

PSHE/PE
- Sun safety
- Create a "Rabbitercise" exercise sequence
- Families - Who lives with you in your house? Who belongs to your family? What is it like living with people of different ages? What helps everybody to get on well with each other?

Useful links

http://www.youtube.com/watch?v=nrO-6fRO8gM

Art
- Draw and paint rabbits
- Paint seasonal background picture

Year 1 Science:
How do the seasons impact on what we do?
Y2 Science:
How can we grow our own salad?

The Learning Challenge CURRICULUM

Author: Emily Gravett
Publisher: Macmillan
ISBN: 978-0-330-50397-6

Planning for Quality Texts: I Love You, Blue Kangaroo

These documents are intended to support the planning of effective literacy units based on high quality books. They are not intended to be lesson plans, but offer a menu of possible ideas for teachers to use as starting points to plan for purposeful learning and give pupils reasons for writing as well as the skills they need to write with impact on their reader. They follow a learning sequence:

- a hook to fully engage and interest the children
- responding to reading activities to allow immersion in and exploration of the text, including picture exploration, book and writer talk
- capturing ideas activities which include drama and talk to support understanding of the text and to develop vocabulary, language and ideas for writing
- possibilities for the contextualised teaching of grammar
- sentence games to develop creativity, vocabulary, language and grammar
- links to guided reading
- a range of writing tasks which may be final unit outcomes or incidental opportunities during the unit

Specific mention is made of the writing sequence:

- modelled writing - teacher models the writing process aloud and the decisions writers make about sentences, paragraphs etc to create impact on the reader. This can also include the modelling of planning and spelling strategies.
- shared writing - collaborative composition with discussion and suggestions about what to write and how to write it to create the intended effect. At this point children may write a sentence/s, often in pairs, on whiteboards which are then discussed.
- guided writing - small group sessions based on specific needs of a specific group of children. The session may address misconceptions, bridge gaps or extend learning and can take place at any point during the unit.

In addition, cross-curricular links are suggested, including links to challenges from the Learning Challenge Curriculum.

Possible Written Outcomes or Incidental Writing Opportunities

- Report on own favourite toy
- Report on favourite toy belonging to parent or grandparent
- Retell the story
- Retell the story from Blue kangaroo's point of view
- Thank you letter from Lily to one of the characters who give her a gift
- Thought/speech bubbles at different points in the story for Blue Kangaroo
- Thought/speech bubbles for other toys during the story or at the end
- Write a different ending
- Note from Blue kangaroo to Lily when he falls out of bed
- Write new version of Ten in the Bed

YEAR 1

Hook

- Message from Lily or Blue kangaroo
- Bring your favourite soft toy day

1. Responding to the Text

- Book talk: Use front cover. What might this book be about? Do you think Blue Kangaroo is the girl's favourite toy? Do you have a favourite toy?
- Book talk: Read to picture of Blue Kangaroo leaving Lily's room. Can you predict what might happen next?
- Book talk: How do we know that the baby likes Blue Kangaroo?
- Book talk: Why can't Blue Kangaroo sleep at night? Has that ever happened to you?
- Book talk: Do you know any other stories about toys that get lost?
- Book talk: Do you think Blue Kangaroo was happy with the baby?
- Book talk: Do you like the ending of the book?
- Writer talk: Can you sort the story into the beginning, the middle and the end?
- Writer talk: Can you say what the problem is in the story?
- Writer talk: Can you spot the adjectives the writer has used? Can you say whether they are good adjectives?

2. Capturing Ideas

- Make a story mountain or story map
- Use the mountain or map to retell the story
- Think of questions to ask Blue Kangaroo
- Hot seat Blue Kangaroo
- Think about how he felt at these different points
- Make a word bank of feelings words and choose a good word for how Blue Kangaroo felt at different points in the story
- Think of some different endings to the story
- Learn Ten in the Bed
- Adapt Ten in the Bed by using the toys in the story or the class' favourite toys and perform
- Discuss how they would feel if they lost their favourite toy or explain how they felt when they lost a favourite toy
- Think about class' favourite toys. Are there different kinds of toys? What makes them different?
- Label a picture/photo of own toy. Add adjectives/adjectival phrases
- Find out about the toys their parents or grandparents had? Talk about the differences. Are toys better now?

Sentence Games (use throughout unit)

- Sentence not a sentence game
- Adjectives with talent games - choosing the best adjectives
- Fortunately, unfortunately game
- Adjectives with talent cline game with feelings words

Guided Reading Possibilities

- Read other Blue Kangaroo books - build on understanding his and Lily's characters and story structure - beginning middle, end.
- Non-fiction books about toys
- Identify and discuss features of text type for final written outcome. Level of text can be pitched at each groups' level, ensuring both access and challenge.

3. Contextualised Grammar Teaching

- Reinforce concept of a sentence
- Choosing effective adjectives
- Sentence with an adjectival phrase to add detail - Lily had a patchwork elephant **with floppy ears.**

4. Modelled Writing
Shared Writing
Guided Writing
Independent Writing

MAKING LINKS ACROSS THE CURRICULUM

Geography/Science/History
- Investigate toys from the past
- Investigate toys from other countries

Maths
- Set up toy shop - price items
- Buying and selling toys

ICT
- Play a computer game and compare it with playing a board game

PSHE
- Are toys today better than toys my grandparents played with?
- Blue Kangaroo is Lily's special toy? What does special mean?
- What do we mean by sharing? Why should we share with others? Is it difficult to share sometimes?

Useful links
http://www.youtube.com/watch?v=BpNML5nkGmo

Art/DT
- Sketch your favourite toy
- Design a new toy for Lily

Year 1 History:
Is a Wii better than grandma and grandpa's toys?

The Learning Challenge
CURRICULUM

Author: Emma Chichester Clark
Publisher: Harper Collins
ISBN: 978-0-006646846

Planning for Quality Texts: Leaf Man

These documents are intended to support the planning of effective literacy units based on high quality books. They are not intended to be lesson plans, but offer a menu of possible ideas for teachers to use as starting points to plan for purposeful learning and give pupils reasons for writing as well as the skills they need to write with impact on their reader. They follow a learning sequence:

- a hook to fully engage and interest the children
- responding to reading activities to allow immersion in and exploration of the text, including picture exploration, book and writer talk
- capturing ideas activities which include drama and talk to support understanding of the text and to develop vocabulary, language and ideas for writing
- possibilities for the contextualised teaching of grammar
- sentence games to develop creativity, vocabulary, language and grammar
- links to guided reading
- a range of writing tasks which may be final unit outcomes or incidental opportunities during the unit

Specific mention is made of the writing sequence:

- modelled writing - teacher models the writing process aloud and the decisions writers make about sentences, paragraphs etc to create impact on the reader. This can also include the modelling of planning and spelling strategies.
- shared writing - collaborative composition with discussion and suggestions about what to write and how to write it to create the intended effect. At this point children may write a sentence/s, often in pairs, on whiteboards which are then discussed.
- guided writing - small group sessions based on specific needs of a specific group of children. The session may address misconceptions, bridge gaps or extend learning and can take place at any point during the unit.

In addition, cross-curricular links are suggested, including links to challenges from the Learning Challenge Curriculum.

YEAR 1

Possible Written Outcomes or Incidental Writing Opportunities

- Instructions - How to make a Leaf Person
- Write or perform We're going on a leaf hunt
- Label different leaves
- Captions or sentences for collected leaves
- Recount of leaf hunt or visit from Leaf Man or Lady
- List things Leaf Man saw in the book
- Sentence to explain meaning of unfamiliar words from book for class glossary
- Write their own story for Leaf Man's travels in school
- Passport for Leaf Man
- Travel wish
- Explain how they made a home for Leaf Man

Hook

- Go on a leaf hunt
- Visit from a leaf man or lady!

1. Responding to the Text

- Visual literacy: Show front cover. Predict what the book might be about.
- Book talk: Who might Leaf Man be? Where might he live? What might he do?
- Book talk: What does it mean that the Leaf Man has no travel plans? Why do you think he has no plans?
- Book talk: What does the writer mean when she says that "where a Leaf Man will land, only the wind knows"?
- Visual literacy: Are the pictures in this book like the pictures in other books? Do you like them?
- Book talk: Do you like this story? Have you got any questions about it?
- Book talk: Are there any words you don't understand? How can we find out what they mean?
- Book talk: Can you spot and read any words we are learning?
- Writer talk: Can you spot any verbs that tell us how Leaf Man was travelling?

2. Capturing Ideas

- Innovate We're going on a bear hunt - We're going on a leaf hunt
- Think of questions to ask Leaf Man
- Hot seat Leaf Man
- Make a leaf man puppet - paper bag with leaves stuck on the outside to make leaf man
- Describe the shape and colour of leaves
- Use senses to think of words about leaves - sight, sound and touch
- Word tree - word bank of words about leaves. Include adjectives and verbs
- Make a class glossary for the unfamiliar words in the book
- Make a story map of Leaf man's travels
- Retell story orally
- Plan a journey through the school/grounds for Leaf Man using a story map
- Add prepositions - through the door, across the hall etc.
- Use Leaf Man puppet to oral tell story of travels round the school using story map
- Make a home for Leaf Man

Sentence Games (use throughout unit)

- Sentence not a sentence game
- Cline game with verbs
- Preposition game

Guided Reading Possibilities

- Other journey stories - We're Going on a Bear Hunt, Rosie's Walk, On the Way Home etc.
- Explore Leaf Man and Red Leaf, Yellow Leaf by Lois Elhert
- Identify and discuss features of text type for final written outcome. Level of text can be pitched at each groups' level, ensuring both access and challenge.

3. Contextualised Grammar Teaching

- Prepositions
- Concept of a sentence
- Strong movement verbs

4. Modelled Writing
Shared Writing
Guided Writing
Independent Writing

MAKING LINKS ACROSS THE CURRICULUM

Geography/Science/History
- Link to Science - seasonal changes
- Match leaves to the trees they come from

Maths
- Shape and size vocabulary to describe leaves
- Directions

ICT
- Take photographs of the different places around school that Leaf Man visits
-
-

PSHE
- Leaf Man does not seem to have a home. Do you think he needs one?

Useful links

Art/DT
- Leaf rubbing
- Leaves to make leaf people or animals

Year 1 Geography: Where do the leaves go in Winter?

The Learning Challenge CURRICULUM

Author: Lois Elhert
Publisher: Harper Collins
ISBN: 978-0-00-749093-6

Planning with Quality Texts: Footprints in the Snow

These documents are intended to support the planning of effective literacy units based on high quality picture books. They are not intended to be lesson plans, but offer a menu of possible ideas for teachers to use as starting points to plan for purposeful learning and give pupils reasons for writing as well as the skills they need to write with impact on their reader. They follow a learning sequence:

- a hook to fully engage and interest the children
- responding to reading activities to allow immersion in and exploration of the text, including picture exploration, book and writer talk
- capturing ideas activities which include drama and talk to support understanding of the text and to develop vocabulary, language and ideas for writing
- possibilities for the contextualised teaching of grammar
- sentence games to develop creativity, vocabulary, language and grammar
- links to guided reading
- a range of writing tasks which may be final unit outcomes or incidental opportunities during the unit

Specific mention is made of the writing sequence:

- modelled writing - teacher models the writing process aloud and the decisions writers make about sentences, paragraphs etc to create impact on the reader. This can also include the modelling of planning and spelling strategies.
- shared writing - collaborative composition with discussion and suggestions about what to write and how to write it to create the intended effect. At this point children may write a sentence/s, often in pairs, on whiteboards which are then discussed.
- guided writing - small group sessions based on specific needs of a specific group of children. The session may address misconceptions, bridge gaps or extend learning and can take place at any point during the unit.

In addition, cross-curricular links are suggested, including links to challenges from the Learning Challenge Curriculum.

YEAR 1 AND 2

Possible Written Outcomes or Incidental Writing Opportunities

- Introduce a new animal and write dialogue between them new animal and wolf
- Speech bubbles for dialogue between
- Write ending to story
- Change the main character and write story
- Fact file/information writing on wolves
- Character profiles of wolf and wolves from other stories
- Description of wolf/labelled picture
- Are wolves always bad?
- Reply to wolf's letter
- Invitation to a tea party to new friend
- Instructions - how to be a good/bad wolf
- Recipe
- Shopping list for recipe

Hook

- Footprint trail inside or outside
- Letter from wolf asking for someone to be his friend

1. Responding to the Text

- Look at first double page. What do all the objects/details in the picture tell us about the wolf?
- **Book talk:** What do you like/dislike about the book?
- **Book talk:** Which other stories about wolves can you find?
- **Book talk:** how do you think the story will end?
- **Book talk:** How are wolves usually portrayed in stories? Is this wolf different? Does he change during the story?
- **Book talk:** do you think wolf fell asleep in the bath and had a dream or did he really write a story?
- **Picture Exploration:** Are there any clues in the pictures that explain the story wolf wrote?
- **Writer talk:** look at how the text is laid out. What impact does that have on the reader?
- **Writer talk:** Why has the writer used capital letters for some words?

2. Capturing Ideas

- Role on the wall of wolf
- Developing questions and hot seating characters
- Look at wolves in other stories: behaviour, actions, descriptions and mind map. Build word bank of commonalities
- Make a wolf's home in role play/reading area with wolf's writing table. What else might wolf write? Shopping list/invitation/note
- What might wolf like to eat to prevent him eating the duck? Research possible recipes and make.
- Make a story map and retell story orally
- Think of other animals the wolf could meet
- Role play meetings between new animals and the wolf
- Match different footprints to animals
- Research wolves under identified headings in groups and share information - rainbow groups/envoy groups.

Sentence Games (use throughout unit)

- Base sentence changed into different sentence types
- Fortunately, unfortunately game to support sentence construction
- Conjunctions game with identified conjunctions as appropriate

Guided Reading Possibilities

- Non-fiction texts on wolves
- Other wolf stories - for example: Clever Polly and the Stupid Wolf - Catherine Storr, Wolves, Wolf Won't Bite - Emily Gravett, The Cultivated Wolf - Becky Bloom
- Identify and discuss features of text type for final written outcome. Level of text can be pitched at each groups' level, ensuring both access and challenge.

3. Contextualised Grammar Teaching

- Using different sentence types with a focus on questions
- Understanding of dialogue through use of speech bubbles or direct speech as appropriate

4. Modelled Writing
Shared Writing
Guided Writing
Independent Writing

MAKING LINKS ACROSS THE CURRICULUM

Geography
- Weather types

Art
- Making footprints and creating footprint trails
- Using prints to make patterns

PSHE
- Making friends - identifying ways to respond to requests for friendship

Useful links
http://www.bear-tracker.com

Science
- Identifying animal prints and matching to different animals and identifying herbivore, carnivore, omnivore and prey or predator

KS1 Science: Why humans are not like tigers?

The Learning Challenge CURRICULUM

Author: Mei Matsuoka
Publisher: Anderson Press
ISBN: 978-1-84270-733-3

Planning for Quality Texts: Beegu

These documents are intended to support the planning of effective literacy units based on high quality picture books. They are not intended to be lesson plans, but offer a menu of possible ideas for teachers to use as starting points to plan for purposeful learning and give pupils reasons for writing as well as the skills they need to write with impact on their reader. They follow a learning sequence:

- a hook to fully engage and interest the children
- responding to reading activities to allow immersion in and exploration of the text, including picture exploration, book and writer talk
- capturing ideas activities which include drama and talk to support understanding of the text and to develop vocabulary, language and ideas for writing
- possibilities for the contextualised teaching of grammar
- sentence games to develop creativity, vocabulary, language and grammar
- links to guided reading
- a range of writing tasks which may be final unit outcomes or incidental opportunities during the unit

Specific mention is made of the writing sequence:

- modelled writing - teacher models the writing process aloud and the decisions writers make about sentences, paragraphs etc to create impact on the reader. This can also include the modelling of planning and spelling strategies.
- shared writing - collaborative composition with discussion and suggestions about what to write and how to write it to create the intended effect. At this point children may write a sentence/s, often in pairs, on whiteboards which are then discussed.
- guided writing - small group sessions based on specific needs of a specific group of children. The session may address misconceptions, bridge gaps or extend learning and can take place at any point during the unit.

In addition, cross-curricular links are suggested, including links to challenges from the Learning Challenge Curriculum.

Possible Written Outcomes or Incidental Writing Opportunities

- Diary entry as Beegu
- Write Beegu 2 - retell the story with added detail in text
- Write Beegu 2 - retell the story with an additional event
- Speech bubbles/dialogue between Beegu and her parents on her return
- Instructions for Beegu to help her understand life on earth
- Explain how a shelter has been made for Beegu
- Postcard to/from Beegu after her return
- Thought bubbles for different events
- Persuade Headteacher to allow Beegu to stay
- Non-chronological report about life on Beegu's planet
- TV report on the sighting of a strange creature

YEAR 1 AND 2

Hook

- Create space ship "crash scene". Children investigate, find clues and take photographs
- Show the beginning of Youtube clip

1. Responding to the Text

- Visual Literacy: use the picture on the front cover – what could this be about?
- Book talk: read sections of story and discuss illustrations. What extra information can we get from them?
- Hot seat Beegu
- Role on the wall for Beegu – add to during book exploration
- Book talk: what do you like or not like about the book?
- Book talk: Have you any questions about the story? Does it remind you of anything?
- Why does no one help Beegu?
- Make emotions graph for Beegu and annotate
- Make story map of events
- Writer talk: There is limited text. How do the illustrations help the reader to understand the story and the characters' feelings?
- Writer talk: How has the writer chosen the information he gives us in the text?

2. Capturing Ideas

- Set up role play area as space ship
- Freeze frame scenes and take photos– thought track and write thought bubbles
- Make story map of events
- Annotate story map with narrative language
- In groups annotate picture of an event in the text to add detail and dialogue as appropriate
- Orally rehearse and write more detailed event
- Use pictures of everyday settings to develop new event. Annotate considering: What would she have seen? What would puzzle her? Who might she meet? What might they do/say? What might Beegu do?
- Add new event to story map and retell in sentences
- Design and make a shelter for Beegu
- Visualise Beegu's home planet. Draw label/annotate

Sentence Games (use throughout unit)

- Sentence not a sentence game based on book
- Conjunctions game
- Improve a sentence- focus on the grammatical elements that need consolidation or review
- Fortunately, unfortunately game
- Chain writing

Guided Reading Possibilities

- Other space stories - Toys in Space - Mini Grey, The Way Back Home – Oliver Jeffers, Dr Xargle's Book of Earthlings - Jeanne Willis, Man on the Moon – Simon Bartram, Here Come the Aliens – Colin McNaughton
- Baboon on the Moon - BFI short film
- Identify and discuss features of text type for final written outcome. Level of text can be pitched at each groups' level, ensuring both access and challenge.

3. Contextualised Grammar Teaching

- Linking words and phrases - Time adverbs/adverbials.
- Linking words and phrases - Ly sentence starters.
- Relative clauses to add detail – noun + who, whom, which or that
- Use of inverted commas for direct speech as appropriate

4. Modelled Writing
Shared Writing
Guided Writing
Independent Writing

MAKING LINKS ACROSS THE CURRICULUM

Geography/Science
- Look at the stars and planets. Make a star map.
- Characteristics and requirements for mammals to live

History
- Space exploration - first trip to the moon

DT/ICT
- Design and build a shelter for Beegu on earth
- Make a book to present story - Beegu 2
- Use Wingdings/symbols to write a message in Beegu's language

PSHE
- Why would no one help Beegu? How could she have been helped?
- Discuss loneliness - watch The Baboon on the Moon. Who might be lonely?
- Was Beegu brave? When have you been brave?

Useful links
http://www.youtube.com/watch?v=no5Sf0MfMZw

Art
- Use night time colours to paint backgrounds - shade and tone
- Create silhouette buildings

Year 1 Science:
What do aliens think of life on planet earth?
Y2 History:
Were Christopher Columbus and Neil Armstrong very brave people?

The Learning Challenge
CURRICULUM

Author: Alexis Deacon
Publisher: Red Fox
ISBN: 978-0-0994174-46

Planning for Quality Texts: The Leopard's Drum

These documents are intended to support the planning of effective literacy units based on high quality picture books. They are not intended to be lesson plans, but offer a menu of possible ideas for teachers to use as starting points to plan for purposeful learning and give pupils reasons for writing as well as the skills they need to write with impact on their reader. They follow a learning sequence:

- a hook to fully engage and interest the children
- responding to reading activities to allow immersion in and exploration of the text, including picture exploration, book and writer talk
- capturing ideas activities which include drama and talk to support understanding of the text and to develop vocabulary, language and ideas for writing
- possibilities for the contextualised teaching of grammar
- sentence games to develop creativity, vocabulary, language and grammar
- links to guided reading
- a range of writing tasks which may be final unit outcomes or incidental opportunities during the unit

Specific mention is made of the writing sequence:

- modelled writing - teacher models the writing process aloud and the decisions writers make about sentences, paragraphs etc to create impact on the reader. This can also include the modelling of planning and spelling strategies.
- shared writing - collaborative composition with discussion and suggestions about what to write and how to write it to create the intended effect. At this point children may write a sentence/s, often in pairs, on whiteboards which are then discussed.
- guided writing - small group sessions based on specific needs of a specific group of children. The session may address misconceptions, bridge gaps or extend learning and can take place at any point during the unit.

In addition, cross-curricular links are suggested, including links to challenges from the Learning Challenge Curriculum.

YEAR 1 AND 2

Possible Written Outcomes or Incidental Writing Opportunities

- Retell story with additional description
- Write story with a different animal outwitting Osebo
- Explain why drums are so important in Ghana
- Fact file on African animal
- Fact file on Ghana
- List of animals' qualities
- Write about own special qualities
- Thought bubbles for each animal at different points in the story
- Use Comic Life to create comic strip version of story. Add captions.
- Add thought and/or speech bubbles to comic strip

Hook

- Have a djembe (African drum) in the classroom. Children discuss what it is and why it might be in their classroom.
- Run a drumming workshop

1. Responding to the Text

- Read the story up to the point where Tortoise is going to try to trick Osebo. Predict what might happen.
- Book talk: Complete story. What do they like or dislike about the story?
- Book talk: does the story remind you of anything? Do you know any other stories like this?
- Book/Writer talk: Discuss the meaning of the adjectives used to describe the characters and relate to their own experience
- Book talk: What else can we find out about each animal from what they say and do? Create spider diagrams for each animal.
- Book talk: Are there any clues about life in Ghana?
- Writer talk: Can you find any language patterns in the story?
- Writer talk: Look at the examples of the use of the power of three in the book. How does this help us to understand the animals' characters?

2. Capturing Ideas

- Role play area set up with objects from story/ stick puppets etc to enable retelling of story
- Make story boxes for different settings with playdough characters
- Make class story map, annotate with key story language and retell story orally
- Create own story map
- Role play exchanges with Osebo/Nyame
- Freeze frame role plays and thought track
- Annotate with adjectives/power of three sentences
- Annotate with time adverbs
- Research African animals/Ghana
- Explore quality/characteristic other animals may have had to outwit Osebo and build vocabulary
- Develop captions for each event and orally rehearse
- Explore the different types of drums used in Ghana

Sentence Games (use throughout unit)

- Sentence not a sentence game based on book
- Generating and ordering adjectives according to intensity
- Dramatising the behaviour of a character using adjective from the text
- Improve a sentence - focus on the grammatical elements that need consolidation or review

Guided Reading Possibilities

- Read other stories set in Africa (Lila and the Secret of Rain, Bringing Rain to Kapiti Plain, Mama Panya's Pancakes, Handa stories). Look for clues to the setting.
- Non-fiction texts on Ghana and/or animals
- Identify and discuss features of text type for final written outcome. Level of text can be pitched at each groups' level, ensuring both access and challenge.

3. Contextualised Grammar Teaching

- Choosing precise adjectives to capture animals' characters
- Using adjectives to create "power of three" sentences for animal
- Time adverbs to sequence events in the story
- Focus on concept of a sentence as needed.

4. Modelled Writing
Shared Writing
Guided Writing
Independent Writing

MAKING LINKS ACROSS THE CURRICULUM

Geography/Science
- Explore how drums make sounds and how they differ according to their size
- Study of Ghana

Maths
- 2D shapes
- Sequential, repeating patterns of 2D shapes

Art
- Look at the traditional patterns in the illustrations and the colours used
- Print geometric patterns in the style of the illustrations

PSHE
- Think about personal qualities of characters and relate to own experiences

Useful links
- http://africa.si.edu/exhibits/animals/cole.html
- http://africa.si.edu/exhibits/animals/ ArtfulAnimalsActivityGuide.pdf

Music/Dance
- Work with different drums
- Beating different rhythms

Year 1 Science:
Why is a human not like a tiger?
Year 2 Geography
Where would you prefer to live: England or Africa?

The Learning Challenge
CURRICULUM

Author: Jessica Souhami
Publisher:
ISBN:

Planning for Quality Texts: Man on the Moon

These documents are intended to support the planning of effective literacy units based on high quality picture books. They are not intended to be lesson plans, but offer a menu of possible ideas for teachers to use as starting points to plan for purposeful learning and give pupils reasons for writing as well as the skills they need to write with impact on their reader. They follow a learning sequence:

- a hook to fully engage and interest the children
- responding to reading activities to allow immersion in and exploration of the text, including picture exploration, book and writer talk
- capturing ideas activities which include drama and talk to support understanding of the text and to develop vocabulary, language and ideas for writing
- possibilities for the contextualised teaching of grammar
- sentence games to develop creativity, vocabulary, language and grammar
- links to guided reading
- a range of writing tasks which may be final unit outcomes or incidental opportunities during the unit

Specific mention is made of the writing sequence:

- modelled writing - teacher models the writing process aloud and the decisions writers make about sentences, paragraphs etc to create impact on the reader. This can also include the modelling of planning and spelling strategies.
- shared writing - collaborative composition with discussion and suggestions about what to write and how to write it to create the intended effect. At this point children may write a sentence/s, often in pairs, on whiteboards which are then discussed.
- guided writing - small group sessions based on specific needs of a specific group of children. The session may address misconceptions, bridge gaps or extend learning and can take place at any point during the unit.

In addition, cross-curricular links are suggested, including links to challenges from the Learning Challenge Curriculum.

Possible Written Outcomes or Incidental Writing Opportunities

- Job description
- Instructions - how to fly to the moon
- Postcard from the moon
- Moon cakes recipe
- Report on created alien for Guide to Intergalactic Aliens
- Rules for visiting the moon
- Poster advertising day trips to the moon
- Speech bubbles/dialogue between aliens
- Comic strip of aliens on the moon when Bob is not there
- Day in the life of children in class
- Day in the life an alien
- Recount of journey to the moon
- Identity card for moon trip
- Ticket for moon trip
- Fact file on astronaut

YEAR 1 AND 2

Hook

- Email from Bob asking for a substitute while he is on holiday
- Picture of Bob in his house as photo with an address on the back. Who could this be?

1. Responding to the Text

- Visual literacy: Use picture of Bob in his home. What can we find out about him/ What might his job be?
- What questions would we like to ask him?
- Visit from Bob to answer the questions
- Visual literacy: Explore other chosen pictures
- Visual literacy: spot the aliens in the illustrations
- Book talk: Does anything about the book puzzle you?
- Book talk: Does the book remind you of anything?
- Book talk: Why does Bob think that there are no such things as aliens?
- Book talk: Do Bob's friends think there are aliens?
- What questions would you like to ask an alien?
- Hot seat an alien
- Story map of Bob's day
- Oral retell of Bob's day
- Writer talk: How is this book written? Is it a story?
- Writer talk: What tense does the writer use? Why?

2. Capturing Ideas

- Set up role play area as Bob's rocket
- Identify key language, model and role play visit to the moon
- List all Bob's jobs
- Story map of aliens' day
- Create bank of time adverbs and adverbials
- Annotate map with different sentence starters, including time adverbs and adverbials
- Oral retell of aliens'day
- Role play interactions between aliens, using pictures in books
- Label picture of alien from book
- Create a word bank of descriptive language for aliens
- Plan an alien party - what would they eat? What would they do? What games might they play?
- Create and draw an alien and label
- Make a story box and create alien story
- Research astronauts and moon exploration

Sentence Games (use throughout unit)

- Sentence not a sentence game based on book
- Conjunctions game
- Improve a sentence- focus on the grammatical elements that need consolidation or review
- Fortunately, unfortunately game
- Chain writing

Guided Reading Possibilities

- Explore other Simon Bartram books about Bob and his adventures
- Non-fiction texts on the moon and space exploration
- Identify and discuss features of text type for final written outcome. Level of text can be pitched at each groups' level, ensuring both access and challenge

3. Contextualised Grammar Teaching

- Use of present tense and present progressive form
- Range of sentence starters, including time adverbs and adverbials - Just as..., To his amazement..., Luckily..., First of all..., Much later...
- Sentence types - statement, question, exclamation
- Adjectival/adverbial phrases to describe aliens - On either side of its head..., with green spots

4. Modelled Writing
Shared Writing
Guided Writing
Independent Writing

MAKING LINKS ACROSS THE CURRICULUM

Geography/Science
- Look at the stars and planets. Make a map or model of the planets

History
- Space exploration - first trip to the moon

DT/ICT
- Day in the life of Bob as TV documentary
- TV advert for a day trip to the moon
-

PSHE
- Discuss bravery and going into the unknown

Useful links
http://www.youtube.com/watch?v=lO_B7CT_-Cs&safe=active
http://www.simonbartram.com/

Art
- Make 3D moonscapes
- Look at use of colour in text. Mix paint to create similar colour palette

Year 1 Science:
What do aliens think of life on planet earth?
Y2 History:
Were Christopher Columbus and Neil Armstrong very brave people?

The Learning Challenge
CURRICULUM

Author: Simon Bartram
Publisher: Templar
ISBN: 978-1840114911

Planning for Quality Texts: The Flower

These documents are intended to support the planning of effective literacy units based on high quality picture books. They are not intended to be lesson plans, but offer a menu of possible ideas for teachers to use as starting points to plan for purposeful learning and give pupils reasons for writing as well as the skills they need to write with impact on their reader. They follow a learning sequence:

- a hook to fully engage and interest the children
- responding to reading activities to allow immersion in and exploration of the text, including picture exploration, book and writer talk
- capturing ideas activities which include drama and talk to support understanding of the text and to develop vocabulary, language and ideas for writing
- possibilities for the contextualised teaching of grammar
- sentence games to develop creativity, vocabulary, language and grammar
- links to guided reading
- a range of writing tasks which may be final unit outcomes or incidental opportunities during the unit

Specific mention is made of the writing sequence:

- modelled writing - teacher models the writing process aloud and the decisions writers make about sentences, paragraphs etc to create impact on the reader. This can also include the modelling of planning and spelling strategies.
- shared writing - collaborative composition with discussion and suggestions about what to write and how to write it to create the intended effect. At this point children may write a sentence/s, often in pairs, on whiteboards which are then discussed.
- guided writing - small group sessions based on specific needs of a specific group of children. The session may address misconceptions, bridge gaps or extend learning and can take place at any point during the unit.

In addition, cross-curricular links are suggested, including links to challenges from the Learning Challenge Curriculum.

Possible Written Outcomes or Incidental Writing Opportunities

- Fact file on flower
- Thought/speech bubbles for Brigg and the shopkeeper
- Retell story or part of story
- Retell of story or part of story in the first person as Brigg
- Write sentences for the illustration on the last page in the book
- Instructions for planting seeds
- Flower diary recording the growth of a seed/plant
- Life cycle of a plant
- Recount of garden centre visit
- Garden centre sign or poster for role play area
- Price list
- Information labels for plants in role play area
- Captions for paintings in the style of Georgia O'Keefe

YEAR 1 AND 2

Hook

- Children enter classroom to find plant pots with flowers around the room
- Visit garden centre

1. Responding to the Text

- Book talk: what do you like or not like about the book?
- Book talk: Have you any questions about the story? Does it remind you of anything?
- Book talk: why do you think there were books in the library marked "Do not read"? Were they dangerous?
- Can you think of any other books that the library might have thought were dangerous and why?
- Book talk: why do you think there were no flowers in the city? What would it be like to live in a world where there were no flowers or plants?
- Visual literacy: look at how the illustrator has used colour. What is coloured and what is black, white and grey? How does this change towards the end of the book? Can you say why?
- Writer talk: look at the page where Brigg is planting and watering the seed. What do you notice about the text? Why do you think the writer did this?
- Writer talk: the story ends with a picture. What do you think will happen?

2. Capturing Ideas

- Think of some questions to ask Brigg in an interview
- Interview Brigg
- Find the main events and make story map
- Retell story in complete sentences
- Emotions graph to track Brigg's feelings through the story
- Role play scene with Brigg and the shopkeeper
- Think of endings for the story
- Choose an ending and tell a partner your idea in sentences
- Set up role play/reading area as garden centre
- Make map or flow chart for visit to garden centre
- Retell in complete sentences
- Find information about a flower or a plant - what it is called, what it looks like and where it grows
- Plant seeds and use correct technical vocabulary
- Use photos of seed planting to sequence the process
- Give spoken instructions - how to plant a seed

Sentence Games (use throughout unit)

- Sentence not a sentence game based on book
- Fortunately, unfortunately game
- Improve a sentence- focus on the grammatical elements that need consolidation or review
- Fortunately, unfortunately game
- Chain writing

Guided Reading Possibilities

- Joseph's Yard by Charles Keeping, Jasper's Beanstalk by Nick Butterworth, Titch by Pat Hutchins
- Information texts on plants and flowers, leaflets, fliers from garden centres
- Identify and discuss features of text type for final written outcome. Level of text can be pitched at each groups' level, ensuring both access and challenge.

3. Contextualised Grammar Teaching

- Time adverbs and adverbials to move events forward or sequence instructions
- Forming questions and command sentences
- Commas in lists

4. Modelled Writing
Shared Writing
Guided Writing
Independent Writing

MAKING LINKS ACROSS THE CURRICULUM

Geography/Science
- Grow plant - bean, sunflower etc
- Conditions for growth
- Plants and flowers from other countries

Maths
- Working with money - finding an amount, giving change, adding amounts in role play garden centre

DT/ICT
- Make flowers and plants to sell in garden centre

PSHE
- What does this book make us think?
- Why should we take care of flowers and plants?

Useful links
http://prod.signedstories.com/story-world/adventure/flower

Art
- Study of Georgia O'Keefe
- Painting flowers in the style of Georgia O'Keefe

Year 1 Science:
Which birds and plants would Little Red Riding Hood find in our park?
Year 2 Science:
How can we grow our own salad?

The Learning Challenge CURRICULUM

Author: John Light
Publisher: Child's Play
ISBN: 978-1-84643-016-9

Planning for Quality Texts: Can't You Sleep, Little Bear?

These documents are intended to support the planning of effective literacy units based on high quality books. They are not intended to be lesson plans, but offer a menu of possible ideas for teachers to use as starting points to plan for purposeful learning and give pupils reasons for writing as well as the skills they need to write with impact on their reader. They follow a learning sequence:

- a hook to fully engage and interest the children
- responding to reading activities to allow immersion in and exploration of the text, including picture exploration, book and writer talk
- capturing ideas activities which include drama and talk to support understanding of the text and to develop vocabulary, language and ideas for writing
- possibilities for the contextualised teaching of grammar
- sentence games to develop creativity, vocabulary, language and grammar
- links to guided reading
- a range of writing tasks which may be final unit outcomes or incidental opportunities during the unit

Specific mention is made of the writing sequence:

- modelled writing - teacher models the writing process aloud and the decisions writers make about sentences, paragraphs etc to create impact on the reader. This can also include the modelling of planning and spelling strategies.
- shared writing - collaborative composition with discussion and suggestions about what to write and how to write it to create the intended effect. At this point children may write a sentence/s, often in pairs, on whiteboards which are then discussed.
- guided writing - small group sessions based on specific needs of a specific group of children. The session may address misconceptions, bridge gaps or extend learning and can take place at any point during the unit.

In addition, cross-curricular links are suggested, including links to challenges from the Learning Challenge Curriculum.

YEAR 1 AND 2

Possible Written Outcomes or Incidental Writing Opportunities

- Retell of story from point of view of Big Bear or Little Bear
- Rewrite of short sections of dialogue with strengthened dialogue verbs
- Instructions - How to fall asleep at bedtime
- Recipe - Special bedtime drink or snack
- Invitation to a "darkness" party
- Speech bubbles for Little and Big Bear in changed situation
- Speech bubbles transferred to direct speech
- Comparative/superlative sentences
- Write changed version of story with new idea
- Fact file on bears
- Non-chronological report on bears

Hook

- Short clip from Monsters Inc
- Table top collection of different light sources

1. Responding to the Text

- Book talk: Use title page. Why do you think Little Bear can't sleep?
- Book talk: Why is Little Bear scared? Can you find clues in the book that show us how scared he is?
- Book talk: Do you know any other books where the main character is scared of something?
- Book talk: How does Big Bear try to help Little Bear?
- Book talk: Why do the different sized lanterns not help Little Bear?
- Book talk: Why do you think that looking at the moon helped Little Bear to fall asleep? Do you think there was any another reason why he fell asleep then?
- Book talk: Do you like this story/ Why or why not?
- Writer talk: Can you find any repeated language? Why do you think the writer has used repetition? Can you think of other stories that use repetition?
- Writer talk: Each time Big Bear gets up the writer uses a different dialogue word. How does this help us to understand how he is feeling?

2. Capturing Ideas

- Role play area set up as a cave
- Make a picture sequence or story map
- Retell story orally from picture sequence or story map
- List other ideas to help Little Bear not to be afraid of the dark
- List other things that Little Bear might be afraid of
- Choose one idea and think how Little Bear's fear could be solved
- Make a story map with the new idea
- Role play the conversations between Little and Big Bear
- Make timeline of class or individual bedtime routine
- Think of things that help them fall asleep
- Make timeline of bedtime routine for Little Bear
- Role play giving bedtime routine instructions to Big Bear to make sure Little goes to sleep
- Research information about bears and find 3 facts to share with a partner or group and across pairs or groups
- Find the most interesting facts to use in a fact file or report

Sentence Games (use throughout unit)

- Sentence not a sentence game
- Cline activity - dialogue verbs
- Dialogue verbs - use base sentence. For example - Can't you sleep, Little Bear? and say the sentence in the manner of the dialogue verb

Guided Reading Possibilities

- Owl Babies or The Owl Who Was Afraid of the Dark for greater challenge
- Non-fiction books on bears
- Identify and discuss features of text type for final written outcome. Level of text can be pitched at each groups' level, ensuring both access and challenge.

3. Contextualised Grammar Teaching

- Reinforce concept of a sentence
- Formation of comparative and superlative adjectives
- Use of dialogue - use of inverted commas and wel-chosen dialogue verbs

4. Modelled Writing
Shared Writing
Guided Writing
Independent Writing

MAKING LINKS ACROSS THE CURRICULUM

Geography/Science/History
- Link to Science in Y1
- Investigating light sources

Maths
- Ordering objects using comparative and superlative language

ICT

PSHE
- Little Bear was scared of the dark. What makes you scared?

Useful links
http://www.bbc.co.uk/learningzone/clips/jackanory-junior-little-bear-stories/11515.html

Art/DT
- Night time pictures

Year 1 Science: Why does it get dark earlier in the Winter?

The Learning Challenge **CURRICULUM**

Author: Martin Waddell
Publisher: Walker Books
ISBN: 978-0744507966

Planning for Quality Texts: Winnie at the Seaside

These documents are intended to support the planning of effective literacy units based on high quality picture books. They are not intended to be lesson plans, but offer a menu of possible ideas for teachers to use as starting points to plan for purposeful learning and give pupils reasons for writing as well as the skills they need to write with impact on their reader. They follow a learning sequence:

- a hook to fully engage and interest the children
- responding to reading activities to allow immersion in and exploration of the text, including picture exploration, book and writer talk
- capturing ideas activities which include drama and talk to support understanding of the text and to develop vocabulary, language and ideas for writing
- possibilities for the contextualised teaching of grammar
- sentence games to develop creativity, vocabulary, language and grammar
- links to guided reading
- a range of writing tasks which may be final unit outcomes or incidental opportunities during the unit

Specific mention is made of the writing sequence:

- modelled writing - teacher models the writing process aloud and the decisions writers make about sentences, paragraphs etc to create impact on the reader. This can also include the modelling of planning and spelling strategies.
- shared writing - collaborative composition with discussion and suggestions about what to write and how to write it to create the intended effect. At this point children may write a sentence/s, often in pairs, on whiteboards which are then discussed.
- guided writing - small group sessions based on specific needs of a specific group of children. The session may address misconceptions, bridge gaps or extend learning and can take place at any point during the unit.

In addition, cross-curricular links are suggested, including links to challenges from the Learning Challenge Curriculum.

Possible Written Outcomes or Incidental Writing Opportunities

- Recipe for a magic potion
- Menu for the ice cream parlour with descriptions of different ice creams
- Instructions - How to build a sandcastle
- Rules/advice for keeping safe in the sun
- Postcard from the seaside
- Retell event/s from Wilbur's point of view
- Thought/speech bubbles for people on beach
- Comic strip with speech bubbles and captions
- Transform comic strip into direct speech
- Eye-witness report by one of the people on the beach
- Rewrite the events on the beach, changing the way in which Winnie gets her broomstick back

YEAR 2

Hook

- Trip to the seaside
- Set up water, sand etc and hold themed day - children come in swimming costumes and have a beach picnic

1. Responding to the Text

- Visual Literacy: use the picture on the front cover without the title visible – where is Winnie? What can you tell about how Winnie is feeling and how Wilbur is feeling?
- Book talk: do you like the story? Why? Why not?
- Book talk: do you know any other stories that are set at the seaside?
- Book talk: what do the people on the beach think about Winnie and Wilbur and what happens? How do you know?
- Writer talk: can you find any examples of where the font or text size is different? Why do you think the writer has done this?
- Writer talk: find the sentences that have conjunctions. Can you say whether they are subordinating or co-ordinating conjunctions?
- Writer talk: the writer often uses the power of three. Can you find some examples? Why do you think she uses the power of three?
- Writer talk: the writer uses short sentences next to each other. Why? Can you find some examples?

2. Capturing Ideas

- Story map
- Add time adverbs to map
- Retell story in complete sentences using story map
- Hot seat Winnie and/or Wilbur
- Freeze frame scenes of visitors on the beach at different points in the story and thought track
- Role play selected scenes from above
- Find questions to ask the people on the beach
- Role play interviewing them
- Add speech bubbles to story map at identified point/s
- Collect ideas about how else Winnie might get her broomstick back
- Change an event on the story map - how Winnie gets her broomstick back
- Retell story with new event in complete sentences using story map

Sentence Games (use throughout unit)

- Sentence not a sentence game based on book
- Conjunctions game
- Improve a sentence- focus on the grammatical elements that need consolidation or review
- Ordering adjectives describing feelings in intensity - shocked, surprised, amazed, bewildered...

Guided Reading Possibilities

- Lucy and Tom at the Seaside by Shirley Hughes. Look at clues that tell you about the setting. Compare with Winnie
- Other Winnie stories.
- Identify and discuss features of text type for final written outcome. Level of text can be pitched at each groups' level, ensuring both access and challenge.

3. Contextualised Grammar Teaching

- Use of dialogue - accurate use of inverted commas
- Time adverbs as sentence starters to move story forward
- Power of three in the style of the writer

4. Modelled Writing
Shared Writing
Guided Writing
Independent Writing

MAKING LINKS ACROSS THE CURRICULUM

Maths
- Set up an ice cream parlour. Role play buying and selling. Prices, finding correct amount, giving change, adding amounts.
-

History/Geography
- Seaside in the past - then and now
- Use Google Earth to journey to the sea

DT/ICT
- Design a menu for the ice cream parlour
- Make ice cream sundaes for shop
- Create a digital postcard

PSHE
- Some of the people on the beach are staring and pointing at Winnie and Wilbur when they arrive? Why? Do you think they are behaving well?
- Sun safety

Useful links
http://winnie-the-witch.com/
http://www.youtube.com/watch?v=3jO5Omszt74

Art
- Take photographs on visit or themed day to make a postcard and change the image on a computer

Year 2 Geography: Why do we love to be beside the seaside?

The Learning Challenge CURRICULUM

Author: Valerie Thomas
Publisher: OUP
ISBN: 978-0-19-272726-8

Planning with Quality Texts: Lila and the Secret of the Rain

These documents are intended to support the planning of effective literacy units based on high quality picture books. They are not intended to be lesson plans, but offer a menu of possible ideas for teachers to use as starting points to plan for purposeful learning and give pupils reasons for writing as well as the skills they need to write with impact on their reader. They follow a learning sequence:

- a hook to fully engage and interest the children
- responding to reading activities to allow immersion in and exploration of the text, including picture exploration, book and writer talk
- capturing ideas activities which include drama and talk to support understanding of the text and to develop vocabulary, language and ideas for writing
- possibilities for the contextualised teaching of grammar
- sentence games to develop creativity, vocabulary, language and grammar
- links to guided reading
- a range of writing tasks which may be final unit outcomes or incidental opportunities during the unit

Specific mention is made of the writing sequence:

- modelled writing - teacher models the writing process aloud and the decisions writers make about sentences, paragraphs etc to create impact on the reader. This can also include the modelling of planning and spelling strategies.
- shared writing - collaborative composition with discussion and suggestions about what to write and how to write it to create the intended effect. At this point children may write a sentence/s, often in pairs, on whiteboards which are then discussed.
- guided writing - small group sessions based on specific needs of a specific group of children. The session may address misconceptions, bridge gaps or extend learning and can take place at any point during the unit.

In addition, cross-curricular links are suggested, including links to challenges from the Learning Challenge Curriculum.

YEAR 2

Possible Written Outcomes or Incidental Writing Opportunities

- Write story with one change
- Character profile of Lila
- Message/note from Lila to her mother
- Retell from Lila's point of view
- Fact file on Kenya or other location
- Comparison of life in Kenya in a village or in Nairobi
- Thought/speech bubbles at different points in the story
- Weather poem - based on one weather type that they have experience of (Rain!)
- Use story boxes to film story with text or voice and sound included

Hook

- Go on a weather walk - observe all the things that we need rain for
- Use first double page of book - see Responding to the Text

1. Responding to the Text

- Use picture on front cover - where do you think this story takes place? Why do you think that?
- Picture exploration: look closely at the first double page without text. What do you think is happening? How would you feel if you were living there? Why is the sun so big?
- Read up to the page where Lila has talked to the sky, but there is still no sign of rain. What else could Lila do? Predict the ending.
- Book talk: are there any questions or reminders in the story
- Book talk/visual literacy: How do the pictures help us to understand how the characters feel?
- Book talk: Think about the title. Why is it the secret of rain? Did Lila really make it rain?
- Writer talk: Can we find any information about village life in Kenya?
- Writer talk: Look at the examples of the use of the power of three in the book. Why has the writer done this?

2. Capturing Ideas

- Role play area set up with objects from story/ stick puppets etc to enable retelling of story
- Make story boxes for different settings with playdough characters
- Make class story map, annotate with key story language and retell story orally
- Hotseat Lila
- Use an emotions graph to track Lilas's feelings across the story and create word bank of feeling words
- Paired role play of conversations between characters (Lila and her mother, Lila and her grandfather, two villagers)
- Create own story map with one change - different main character, different "secret", different setting (if part of the unit is to look at other localities).
- Research Kenya/other localities
- Develop vocabulary around the sun and hot weather and other weather types

Sentence Games (use throughout unit)

- Sentence not a sentence game based on book
- Preposition poem - Above the sun is…, Below the sun is… etc
- Similes game - The sun is like…/The rain is like…
- Improve a sentence - focus on the grammatical elements that need consolidation or review

Guided Reading Possibilities

- Read other stories set in Africa (The Leopard's Drum, Bringing Rain to Kapiti Plain, Mama Panya's Pancakes, Handa stories). Look for clues to the setting.
- Non-fiction texts on Kenya and/or other locations
- Identify and discuss features of text type for final written outcome. Level of text can be pitched at each groups' level, ensuring both access and challenge.

3. Contextualised Grammar Teaching

- Use of similes as in text and developing others
- Using "power of three" sentences in text as a model, create own sentences
- Use of dialogue in a story and how to use inverted commas
- Focus on concept of a sentence as needed.

4. Modelled Writing
Shared Writing
Guided Writing
Independent Writing

MAKING LINKS ACROSS THE CURRICULUM

Geography/Science
- Look at the effects of weather on life
- Habitats - how plants and animals survive
- Study of Kenya or other location

Art
- Create backgrounds in boxes in the style of the story illustrations
- Make clay /playdough figures in the style of the story

PSHE
- Lila had a lot of courage because she did not give up even though she was in a desperate situation. Do you know of anyone like Lila? Reflect on their own experiences of being courageous and of not giving up when things are difficult.
- Could the world ever run out of water? How can we save water?

Useful links
- www.kora-music.com/
- www.youtube.com/watch?v=BXvKJKUtPKI

Music/Dance
- Listen and respond to Kenyan music
- Create rain music and a rain dance

Year 2 Geography
Where would you prefer to live: England or Africa?

The Learning Challenge
CURRICULUM

Author: David Conway
Publisher: Francis Lincoln Children's Books
ISBN: 978-1847800350

Planning with Quality Texts: Meerkat Mail

These documents are intended to support the planning of effective literacy units based on high quality picture books. They are not intended to be lesson plans, but offer a menu of possible ideas for teachers to use as starting points to plan for purposeful learning and give pupils reasons for writing as well as the skills they need to write with impact on their reader. They follow a learning sequence:

- a hook to fully engage and interest the children
- responding to reading activities to allow immersion in and exploration of the text, including picture exploration, book and writer talk
- capturing ideas activities which include drama and talk to support understanding of the text and to develop vocabulary, language and ideas for writing
- possibilities for the contextualised teaching of grammar
- sentence games to develop creativity, vocabulary, language and grammar
- links to guided reading
- a range of writing tasks which may be final unit outcomes or incidental opportunities during the unit

Specific mention is made of the writing sequence:

- modelled writing - teacher models the writing process aloud and the decisions writers make about sentences, paragraphs etc to create impact on the reader. This can also include the modelling of planning and spelling strategies.
- shared writing - collaborative composition with discussion and suggestions about what to write and how to write it to create the intended effect. At this point children may write a sentence/s, often in pairs, on whiteboards which are then discussed.
- guided writing - small group sessions based on specific needs of a specific group of children. The session may address misconceptions, bridge gaps or extend learning and can take place at any point during the unit.

In addition, cross-curricular links are suggested, including links to challenges from the Learning Challenge Curriculum.

Possible Written Outcomes or Incidental Writing Opportunities

- Postcard
- Email
- Thought/speech bubbles
- Fact file on meerkats
- Report on meerkats
- Letter to relative once he has returned home
- Newspaper report
- Passport/Identity card
- Label
- List
- Restaurant menu

YEAR 1,2,3 AND 4

Hook

- Postcard from Sunny to class
- Role play travelling to Africa and exploring
- Watch Meerkat Manor

1. Responding to the Text

- Watch clips from Meerkat Manor
- Picture exploration: Predicting possibilities, capture page in 2 adjectives, 2 verbs, 2 adverbs, turn the volume up - what might you hear?
- Story map/timeline of events or mapping journey
- Book talk: likes, dislikes, puzzles and reminders
- Writer talk: How does Emily Gravett show the reader how Sunny is feeling and his response to his adventures?
- Writer talk: How is the text organised?
- Writer talk: What types of sentences has Emily Gravett used? What is the effect?
- Writer talk: Look at word choices

2. Capturing Ideas

- Role play each visit
- Freeze frame role plays at different points
- Hot seat Sunny at different points in the story
- Back to back telephone call to family member
- Explore Sunny's feelings at different points in the story
- Make emotion graph to plot rise and fall of feelings
- Annotate graph with synonyms and use in explanatory sentence
- Generate when/where/how adverbials and annotate story map/timeline with possibilities
- Watch David Attenborough interviewing animal expert and identify question types and formal sentence structures for responses
- Role play interviewer/meerkat expert interview(could be filmed and evaluated)

Sentence Games (use throughout unit)

- Conjunctions game
- Warming up the word - generating synonyms for Sunny's feelings
- Improve a basic sentence using Emily Gravett's techniques
- Chain writing with "meerkats" as starting point. Develop according to grammar focus of unit and/or consolidation and practise of prior learning

Guided Reading Possibilities

- Read and explore other books by Emily Gravett and compare to Meerkat Mail
- Identify and discuss features of text type for final written outcome. Level of text can be pitched at each groups' level, ensuring both access and challenge.

3. Contextualised Grammar Teaching

- Explore use of comparative and superlative in text and how these are formed. Generate others from vocabulary generated by previous activities
- Develop expanded noun phrases
- Text is written in the present tense - explore changing to past tense. Investigation into past tense formation
- Use generated adverbials to experiment with creating different effects in sentences

4. Modelled Writing
Shared Writing
Guided Writing
Independent Writing

MAKING LINKS ACROSS THE CURRICULUM

Geography

- Use atlas/globe to find continent where meerkats live. Identify other continents.
- Use Google Earth to look at the places Sunny visits.
- Find places where meerkats could not live and look at location on globe/atlas
- How might you travel to any of these places?
- Which animals might you see?
- What food might you eat?

Science

- Investigate meerkat habitat
- Investigate other habitats and consider why they are suitable for particular creatures

Useful Links

- www.emilygravett.com
- www.animalplanet.co.uk
- http://www.literacyshed.com/the-photostory-shed.html
- www.earth.google.com

PSHE

- What do the meerkats in the story do?
- How is the meerkat family like a human family?
- Why are homes and families important to the meerkats and to us?
- Look at the meerkats' motto.
- What do you think Sunny thinks of the motto at the start of the story?
  How have his feelings changed by the end?
- Create a class motto

Year 1 Geography: Why can't a meerkat live at the north pole?

The Learning Challenge CURRICULUM

Author: Emily Gravett
Publisher: Macmillan Children's Books
ISBN: 978-1405090759

Planning for Quality Texts: The Tin Forest

These documents are intended to support the planning of effective literacy units based on high quality picture books. They are not intended to be lesson plans, but offer a menu of possible ideas for teachers to use as starting points to plan for purposeful learning and give pupils reasons for writing as well as the skills they need to write with impact on their reader. They follow a learning sequence:

- a hook to fully engage and interest the children
- responding to reading activities to allow immersion in and exploration of the text, including picture exploration, book and writer talk
- capturing ideas activities which include drama and talk to support understanding of the text and to develop vocabulary, language and ideas for writing
- possibilities for the contextualised teaching of grammar
- sentence games to develop creativity, vocabulary, language and grammar
- links to guided reading
- a range of writing tasks which may be final unit outcomes or incidental opportunities during the unit

Specific mention is made of the writing sequence:

- modelled writing - teacher models the writing process aloud and the decisions writers make about sentences, paragraphs etc to create impact on the reader. This can also include the modelling of planning and spelling strategies.
- shared writing - collaborative composition with discussion and suggestions about what to write and how to write it to create the intended effect. At this point children may write a sentence/s, often in pairs, on whiteboards which are then discussed.
- guided writing - small group sessions based on specific needs of a specific group of children. The session may address misconceptions, bridge gaps or extend learning and can take place at any point during the unit.

In addition, cross-curricular links are suggested, including links to challenges from the Learning Challenge Curriculum.

KS1 AND LKS2

Possible Written Outcomes or Incidental Writing Opportunities

- Description of selected pictures from book
- Thought bubbles for old man at different points in the book
- Prequel to story - old man's life before he came to the rubbish dump
- Letter to an advice column
- Reply from advice column
- Poster for recycling
- Job advert for a helper for the old man
- Diary entry in role as old man
- Letter from old man about how he used the rubbish to make the forest
- My dream or hope for the future is... to put into class book of dreams
- Description of created environment based on different dreams
- List poem - In the forest of dreams...

Hook

- Boxes of recyclable material in classroom. Challenge children to make a plant or flower.
- Earth Song by Michael Jackson

1. Responding to the Text

- Visual literacy: use small picture on title page. Predict what the book might be about.
- Book talk: why does the old man make a forest from the rubbish?
- Book talk: what problems does the old man have?
- Book talk: what themes are in the book? (loneliness, loss, hope, perseverance)
- Book talk: what message is the writer trying to give the reader?
- Visual Literacy: how does the illustrator help the reader to understand how the forest became real?
- Book talk: why do you think the birds returned?
- Book talk: how do you feel at the end of the book? Can you explain your feelings?
- Writer talk: look at first sentence in book. What effect does she create? How does she do it?
- Writer talk: how does the writer use repeated language? What is the effect?

2. Capturing Ideas

- Think of questions to ask old man - life before he came to the dump, his hopes and dreams
- Hot seat old man
- Annotate pictures with nouns. Add detail - adjectives, verbs, adverbs etc
- Discuss own hopes and dreams
- The forest is the old man's dream. Collect ideas about how an environment would look with a different dream
- Visualise and sketch alternative environment
- Annotate as above
- Listen to or watch guided tour and identify language and "voice" used
- In role as guide, give guided tour to forest in book or new forest of dreams using the above
- Phone call to helpline for advice
- Role play a day in the life of the old man - list the jobs he does
- Interview candidates for job as helper to the old man
- Investigate school and local recycling procedures

Sentence Games (use throughout unit)

- Prepositions game
- Improve a sentence- focus on the grammatical elements that need consolidation or review
- Poetic sentences - In the forest of dreams...
- Chain writing

Guided Reading Possibilities

- A Child's Garden by Michael Foreman, Dinosaurs and All That Rubbish by Michael Foreman, The Flower by John Light. Look at similar themes and messages.
- Posters and leaflets on recycling
- Identify and discuss features of text type for final written outcome. Level of text can be pitched at each groups' level, ensuring both access and challenge.

3. Contextualised Grammar Teaching

- Expanded noun phrases
- Prepositions/prepositional phrases
- Adverbials of place
- Use of repeated language - words, phrases, clauses - and effects they create

4. Modelled Writing
Shared Writing
Guided Writing
Independent Writing

MAKING LINKS ACROSS THE CURRICULUM

Geography/Science
- Recycling
- Ecology
- Food chains

DT/ICT
- Use pictures from book or photographs of new created environment to make slide show
- Add voice over or commentary to make audio guide to the forest

PSHE
- Dreams and aspirations

Useful links

http://vimeo.com/36088583

http://www.literacyshed.com/the-photostory-shed.html

Art
- Make plants/flowers/animals or birds etc from recyclable materials to create a class "Tin Forest"
- Transform plastic pots into plant pots using collage techniques

Year 2 Science:
What is our school made of?
Year 3 Science:
How did that blossom become an apple?
Year 4 Science:
Which wild animals and plants thrive in your locality?

The Learning Challenge
CURRICULUM

Author: Helen Ward
Publisher: Templar
ISBN: 978-1-84011-743-1

KEY STAGE 2 MENUS

KEY STAGE 2 MENUS

Planning with Quality Texts: Fox

These documents are intended to support the planning of effective literacy units based on high quality picture books. They are not intended to be lesson plans, but offer a menu of possible ideas for teachers to use as starting points to plan for purposeful learning and give pupils reasons for writing as well as the skills they need to write with impact on their reader. They follow a learning sequence:

- a hook to fully engage and interest the children
- responding to reading activities to allow immersion in and exploration of the text, including picture exploration, book and writer talk
- capturing ideas activities which include drama and talk to support understanding of the text and to develop vocabulary, language and ideas for writing
- possibilities for the contextualised teaching of grammar
- sentence games to develop creativity, vocabulary, language and grammar
- links to guided reading
- a range of writing tasks which may be final unit outcomes or incidental opportunities during the unit

Specific mention is made of the writing sequence:

- modelled writing - teacher models the writing process aloud and the decisions writers make about sentences, paragraphs etc to create impact on the reader. This can also include the modelling of planning and spelling strategies.
- shared writing - collaborative composition with discussion and suggestions about what to write and how to write it to create the intended effect. At this point children may write a sentence/s, often in pairs, on whiteboards which are then discussed.
- guided writing - small group sessions based on specific needs of a specific group of children. The session may address misconceptions, bridge gaps or extend learning and can take place at any point during the unit.

In addition, cross-curricular links are suggested, including links to challenges from the Learning Challenge Curriculum.

Possible Written Outcomes or Incidental Writing Opportunities

- Writing in role at a particular point in the story
- Diary entry
- Prequel to the story
- Character profile
- Fact file on fox/magpie/dog
- Argument - Dog should have stopped magpie from going with fox
- Fire - friend or foe?
- Newspaper report of event
- Explanation/report on fires
- Final chapter
- 5 line poem based on one page
- Write a new version in the aftermath of a blizzard or a flood

YEAR 3,4,5 AND 6

Hook

- Video footage of forest on fire
- Pose question - Can enemies ever be friends?

1. Responding to the Text

- Use front cover or other picture to predict what might be happening
- Book talk: likes, dislikes, puzzles and reminders
- Writer talk/Visual literacy: Look at the font used and the changing layout of the text? What is the effect of this? What is the effect of the use of colours?
- Visual literacy: look at how the magpie is represented through the story. Consider how the image of Fox and its eyes is used.
- Writer talk: How is the story structured? Plot opening, build up, problem and resolution. Does the story have a complete ending?
- Writer talk/Visual literacy: consider how both text and pictures show what is happening on the left page and introduces something new on the right. Is this also true of the sentences?

2. Capturing Ideas

- Discuss the three characters and build word banks. How do they view each other?
- Hot seat the characters
- Freeze frame key points in the story. How do the characters feel? How do they feel about each other?
- Research forest fires/floods/snow storms
- *What if* activity to develop ideas about what could happen in blizzard or flood setting
- Role play prequel/new ending
- Conscience alley - should dog have welcomed fox?/should dog have stopped magpie from going with fox?
- Role on the wall for characters
- Annotate graph with synonyms and use in explanatory sentence
- Role play television report of fire/flood etc
- Soundscape of story (use Audacity)

Sentence Games (use throughout unit)

- Complex sentence game
- Generate similes/metaphors for characters based on *He flickers through the trees like a tongue of fire.*
- Add detail to a sentence according to year group requirements: for example adding phrases, adding a relative clause
- Experiment with different sentence starters using a basic sentence: *Dog runs through the scrub.*

Guided Reading Possibilities

- Look at other narrative plot structures and compare with Fox
- Identify sentence types from grammar work and look at effect
- Identify and discuss features of text type for final written outcome. Level of text can be pitched at each groups' level, ensuring both access and challenge.

3. Contextualised Grammar Teaching

- Identify present tense verbs: rewrite passages in past tense and investigate past tense forms
- Look at word and language choices linked to heat and fire. Use images of frozen or flooded landscape and generate words and phrases and build to sentences as author's model
- Look at different sentence types used and the effect of these. Focus on year group requirement: complex sentences/fronted adverbials/ing clauses/ed clauses

4. Modelled Writing
Shared Writing
Guided Writing
Independent Writing

MAKING LINKS ACROSS THE CURRICULUM

Geography/Science
- Natural disasters and their impact
- Effect of fire on the earth and trees and plants
- Identifying locations where fires often occur
- Investigate the impact of the weather on fires in these locations

Art
- Painting using line and colour and cross-hatching to create own illustrations
- Using charcoal to create outlines
- Study of eyes in art and how artists use the eye to draw an observer in to a painting

PSHE
- Explore the idea of friendship and loyalty
- Relate to own experiences of friendship
- Think about magpie and how her character changes and becomes stronger. Relate to other contexts

Music/Dance
- Create a soundscape using ICT or musical instruments
- Show the characters in movement
- Create a movement sequence that shows how magpie changes during the story

KS2 Geography: What makes the earth angry?

The Learning Challenge
CURRICULUM

Author: Margaret Wild
Publisher: Allen and Unwin
ISBN: 978-1864489330

Planning with Quality Texts: The Lost Happy Endings

These documents are intended to support the planning of effective literacy units based on high quality picture books. They are not intended to be lesson plans, but offer a menu of possible ideas for teachers to use as starting points to plan for purposeful learning and give pupils reasons for writing as well as the skills they need to write with impact on their reader. They follow a learning sequence:

- a hook to fully engage and interest the children
- responding to reading activities to allow immersion in and exploration of the text, including picture exploration, book and writer talk
- capturing ideas activities which include drama and talk to support understanding of the text and to develop vocabulary, language and ideas for writing
- possibilities for the contextualised teaching of grammar
- sentence games to develop creativity, vocabulary, language and grammar
- links to guided reading
- a range of writing tasks which may be final unit outcomes or incidental opportunities during the unit

Specific mention is made of the writing sequence:

- modelled writing - teacher models the writing process aloud and the decisions writers make about sentences, paragraphs etc to create impact on the reader. This can also include the modelling of planning and spelling strategies.
- shared writing - collaborative composition with discussion and suggestions about what to write and how to write it to create the intended effect. At this point children may write a sentence/s, often in pairs, on whiteboards which are then discussed.
- guided writing - small group sessions based on specific needs of a specific group of children. The session may address misconceptions, bridge gaps or extend learning and can take place at any point during the unit.

In addition, cross-curricular links are suggested, including links to challenges from the Learning Challenge Curriculum.

YEAR 3,4,5 AND 6

Possible Written Outcomes or Incidental Writing Opportunities

- Diary entries before the happy endings were stolen and after they were stolen
- Thought bubbles for Jub at key points
- Job description for helper for Jub
- Celebrity profile for magazine of Jub/witch
- Description of witch
- Description of alternative "villain"
- New golden pen story based on alternative villain
- Unhappy endings for other traditional tales
- Description of setting - the forest at night
- Eye-witness report
- Newspaper/TV report - Happy Endings Stolen!

Hook

- Happy endings from story distributed around classroom
- Voice mail from character from traditional story asking for help

1. Responding to the Text

- **Book talk:** From first page, begin role on the wall activity - what do we know about Jub? What would we like to know?
- **Book talk:** What do you like/dislike about the book? Are there any puzzles or reminders in the book?
- **Book talk:** What if Jub had not saved the happy endings?
- **Picture exploration:** What is the effect of the gold lettering and stars?
- **Picture exploration:** Look at how the illustrator has portrayed Jub. What does this tell us about her?
- **Picture exploration:** look at picture of Jub in her tree house. What items are there? What might this tell us about her?
- **Writer talk:** How do the pictures help to enhance the text?
- **Writer talk:** In groups take sections of story and highlight descriptive language. What types of language are being used? Choose images and illustrate
- **Writer talk:** Can we find examples of traditional story language? What happens when Jub uses the golden pen?

2. Capturing Ideas

- Role on the wall for Jub developed from activity based on first page
- Identify key points in the story and discuss Jub's thoughts at each point
- Developing questions to ask eye-witness
- Role play interview with eye-witness
- If you were Jub, what would you want in your tree house and why?
- Watch celebrity interviews and questions asked. Develop questions to interview Jub/witch.
- Role play interview using identified questions and sentence starters for responses
- Visit forest/wooded area: What do they feel? What might they feel at night? Complete senses grid
- Create a soundscape for the forest at night
- Gather words and phrases for the forest at night
- In pairs/groups choose alternative villain and, based on the witch, develop language and present orally. Children evaluate and vote on most effective

Sentence Games (use throughout unit)

- Metaphor game: select nouns from story e.g. *forest, trees, stars, sky - trees are coat stands with no coats/many fingered hands reaching for the stars etc*
- What if: using modality. If or when clauses, followed by clause with modal verb - *If the glass slipper was too small for Cinderella, she would not have married the prince etc*
- What am I like? (similes) - *stars like jewelled pins/fiery beams eying the world etc*
- Complex sentence game - *When the last ending was out of the sack, Jub would scamper her way homewards.*
- Improve a sentence - focus on the grammatical elements that need consolidation or review

Guided Reading Possibilities

- Other books by Carol Ann Duffy - The Princesses' Blankets, The Tear Thief
- Range of traditional stories by different authors
- Identify and discuss features of text type for final written outcome. Level of text can be pitched at each groups' level, ensuring both access and challenge.

3. Contextualised Grammar Teaching

- Use of simile and metaphor
- Modal verbs
- Complex sentences
- Paragraph openers and connections between

4. Modelled Writing
Shared Writing
Guided Writing
Independent Writing

MAKING LINKS ACROSS THE CURRICULUM

History
- Historical perspective of traditional and fairy tales

Art/Music
- Create story boxes for the forest
- Make a dance for the witch
- Capture key moments from the story in movement tableaux

PSHE
- Qualities - bravery, courage, resilience in the face of difficulty

Useful links
- http://vimeo.com/7382454
- http://www.eastoftheweb.com/short-stories/Collections/ClasFair.shtml
- http://hca.gilead.org.il/

The Learning Challenge CURRICULUM

Author: Carol Ann Duffy
Publisher: Bloomsbury Children's Books
ISBN: 978-0-7475-8106-2

Planning for Quality Texts: The Village that Vanished

These documents are intended to support the planning of effective literacy units based on high quality picture books. They are not intended to be lesson plans, but offer a menu of possible ideas for teachers to use as starting points to plan for purposeful learning and give pupils reasons for writing as well as the skills they need to write with impact on their reader. They follow a learning sequence:

- a hook to fully engage and interest the children
- responding to reading activities to allow immersion in and exploration of the text, including picture exploration, book and writer talk
- capturing ideas activities which include drama and talk to support understanding of the text and to develop vocabulary, language and ideas for writing
- possibilities for the contextualised teaching of grammar
- sentence games to develop creativity, vocabulary, language and grammar
- links to guided reading
- a range of writing tasks which may be final unit outcomes or incidental opportunities during the unit

Specific mention is made of the writing sequence:

- modelled writing - teacher models the writing process aloud and the decisions writers make about sentences, paragraphs etc to create impact on the reader. This can also include the modelling of planning and spelling strategies.
- shared writing - collaborative composition with discussion and suggestions about what to write and how to write it to create the intended effect. At this point children may write a sentence/s, often in pairs, on whiteboards which are then discussed.
- guided writing - small group sessions based on specific needs of a specific group of children. The session may address misconceptions, bridge gaps or extend learning and can take place at any point during the unit.

In addition, cross-curricular links are suggested, including links to challenges from the Learning Challenge Curriculum.

Possible Written Outcomes or Incidental Writing Opportunities

- Prayer of thanks to ancestors/commemorate survival
- Conversations between ancestors at key points in story
- Retell events from different main characters' point of view or from ancestors' point of view
- Report on slavery
- Instructions for making African hut
- Persuasion text - Chimwale to leave with the villagers
- Discussion text from oral debate - What makes a hero/heroine?
- Information text on Yao people.
- Poem based on illustrations of crossing the river using The Sound Collector as a model

YEAR 3,4,5 AND 6

Hook

- Materials to make an African hut in classroom. Challenge to construct hut.

1. Responding to the Text

- Book talk: What do you like/dislike about the book? Are there any puzzles or reminders in the book?
- Book talk: How has the story been written? How do we know? (Evidence from text and pictures)
- Book talk: What is the role of the ancestors?
- Picture exploration: Use the first picture of the village. What information does this give about the context of the story?
- Picture exploration: Look at the picture of the confrontation with the slavers. How has the illustrator depicted the tension of the situation?
- Picture exploration: Look at the pictures of the villagers crossing the river. What sounds might be heard?
- Writer talk: How do the pictures help to enhance the text?
- Writer talk: In groups look closely at identified pages and find story telling language
- Writer talk: What are the themes in the book?

2. Capturing Ideas

- Map the village and the surrounding area
- Annotate map with words and phrases from text
- Identify story telling language and list. Compare with language in other traditional tales
- Look at a familiar story and create oral version adding oral story telling language
- Retell story using oral story telling language. Perform and video. Evaluate effectiveness of language.
- Role play village meeting where the people are deciding what to do
- Conscience alley - should Grandmother stay or go?
- What is heroism?: note qualities of 3 main characters with evidence from text and pictures
- Debate - what makes a hero? Focus also on use of discursive and persuasive language. Children evaluate use of language
- Research the Yao people
- Research slavery
- Use pictures of villagers crossing river. Create soundscape (instruments/Audacity). Develop bank of phrases (the sighing of the reeds, the shrieking of the children). Develop simile/metaphor

Sentence Games (use throughout unit)

- Chain writing with a focus on impact of adverbials at the beginning
- Play with sound phrases developed to create poetic sentences
- Similes game - The sun is like…
- Metaphor game - The sun is…
- Improve a sentence - focus on the grammatical elements that need consolidation or review

Guided Reading Possibilities

- Read other stories set in Africa
- Listen to/watch oral retellings - focus on the difference between oral and written
- Read The Sound Collector by Roger McGough. Explore use of language.
- Non-fiction texts on slavery
- Identify and discuss features of text type for final written outcome. Level of text can be pitched at each groups' level, ensuring both access and challenge.

3. Contextualised Grammar Teaching

- Opening sentences of paragraphs to indicate a change of time or place - when and where adverbials
- Use of dialogue in narrative - correct use of inverted commas and comma between direct speech and reporting clause
- Persuasive language and its use in narrative and non-narrative texts

4. Modelled Writing
Shared Writing
Guided Writing
Independent Writing

MAKING LINKS ACROSS THE CURRICULUM

Geography/Science
- The villagers dismantled their homes. What materials did they use that made this possible? Why might they have used these materials? Compare to other homes and the materials used.
- Research tribes in African regions

History
- Look at the slave trade in Africa

Art
- Kadir Nelson is an African American artist. Look at some of his other work and find out about the techniques he uses.
- Create illustration or portrait in his style - detailed drawing and a few carefully chosen, rich colours

PSHE
- The qualities faith, courage and sacrifice are picked out by the storyteller. How are they shown? When else might the same qualities be seen?

Useful links
http://www.bbc.co.uk/learningzone/clips/roger-mcgough-the-sound-collector-poem-only/8836.html
http://www.teachingbooks.net/content/interviews/KadirNelson_qu.pdf

The Learning Challenge
CURRICULUM

Author: Ann Grifalconi
Publisher: Ragged Bears Publishing
ISBN-13: 978-1-85714-407-9

Planning for Quality Texts: Wolves in the Walls

These documents are intended to support the planning of effective literacy units based on high quality picture books. They are not intended to be lesson plans, but offer a menu of possible ideas for teachers to use as starting points to plan for purposeful learning and give pupils reasons for writing as well as the skills they need to write with impact on their reader. They follow a learning sequence:

- a hook to fully engage and interest the children
- responding to reading activities to allow immersion in and exploration of the text, including picture exploration, book and writer talk
- capturing ideas activities which include drama and talk to support understanding of the text and to develop vocabulary, language and ideas for writing
- possibilities for the contextualised teaching of grammar
- sentence games to develop creativity, vocabulary, language and grammar
- links to guided reading
- a range of writing tasks which may be final unit outcomes or incidental opportunities during the unit

Specific mention is made of the writing sequence:

- modelled writing - teacher models the writing process aloud and the decisions writers make about sentences, paragraphs etc to create impact on the reader. This can also include the modelling of planning and spelling strategies.
- shared writing - collaborative composition with discussion and suggestions about what to write and how to write it to create the intended effect. At this point children may write a sentence/s, often in pairs, on whiteboards which are then discussed.
- guided writing - small group sessions based on specific needs of a specific group of children. The session may address misconceptions, bridge gaps or extend learning and can take place at any point during the unit.

In addition, cross-curricular links are suggested, including links to challenges from the Learning Challenge Curriculum.

Possible Written Outcomes or Incidental Writing Opportunities

- Sequel to story with different creatures in the walls
- Persuasive text - Lucy trying to convince her family that there are wolves/different animals in the walls
- Sentence sequence based on model in book of different places to live
- Postcard from one of the suggested places in book or from additional ideas
- New blurb for book which gives clues about the story
- Additional text for pages where text is limited: "the wolves came out of the walls", "They huddled at the bottom of the garden that night."
- Alternative scenario following the point where Lucy has returned to the house and is about to be discovered by the wolves
- Retell story from the point of view of pig-puppet
- Newspaper report on the family being forced to leave their home by wolves or wolves rightfully winning back their home (bias)
- Letter from wolf to mother about life in the walls

YEAR 3,4,5 AND 6

Hook

- Torn, incomplete note from Lucy asking for help
- Wallpaper with eyeholes cut out stuck round the room

1. Responding to the Text

- Visual Literacy: use the picture on the front cover – what could this be about?
- Book talk: read sections of story and discuss illustrations
- Book talk: what do you like or not like about the book?
- Book talk: have you any questions about the story? Does it remind you of anything?
- Role on the wall for each of the family – build on these as the book is explored. What do we learn about each of the characters by what they say and how they act?
- How do the characters change during the story?
- Writer talk: find all the verbs that can be linked to fear. How are they used to build tension?
- Writer talk: what techniques has the writer used? What is their effect? (Repetition, alliteration, onomatopoeia, expanded noun phrases, specific verbs and adjectives)
- Writer talk: use selected pages and look at how the writer has used different fonts, text size, colour and bold for different aspects - family/wolves, dialogue/action/description. What is the impact?
- Read pages from the text aloud, changing volume, tone and expression in line with the font type and content

2. Capturing Ideas

- Create a soundscape for the noises inside the walls
- Consider other places the family could live in and add possible information/details
- Develop possible alternative scenarios for what happens when Lucy is about to be discovered by the wolves
- Hot seat a wolf
- Interview family member/s/wolf
- Create plan for alternative animal in the walls:
  -sounds made, focusing on using verbs as nouns
  -family reactions
  -what animals might do when they invade the house
- Review the book, giving recommendations about who might be a suitable audience
- Perform sections of the story
- Role play Lucy trying to persuade each family member that there are creatures in the walls

Sentence Games (use throughout unit)

- List poem - In the walls I heard… (verbs used as nouns and expanded noun phrases
- Complex sentence game
- Improve a sentence based on picture and sentence from book- focus on the grammatical elements that need consolidation or review

Guided Reading Possibilities

- Read and compare other Neil Gaiman books - The Day I Swapped My Dad for 2 Goldfish, Crazy Hair
- Consider structure - hero faces fear and overcomes it. Look at other similar texts.
- Identify and discuss features of text type for final written outcome. Level of text can be pitched at each groups' level, ensuring both access and challenge.

3. Contextualised Grammar Teaching

- Explore how words often used as verbs are used as nouns - howling, yowling, gnawing etc. and build bank of others
- Onomatopoeia - what noises might other animals make?
- Look at how writer has used expanded noun phrases - "little apple-pies with astonishingly hot filling", "second-best tuba", "severe jam damage" and write own based on words to be used in outcome
- Use writer's model of alternative places to live to write own sentences

4. Modelled Writing
Shared Writing
Guided Writing
Independent Writing

MAKING LINKS ACROSS THE CURRICULUM

Geography	Science	ICT
• Investigate places and climates in the world where the family could live	• Study of wolves and their habitat	• Experiment with different fonts and positioning on page to create different effects
PSHE • Lucy overcomes her fear in the story? What are you afraid of? Have you been able to overcome a particular fear?		**Useful links** http://www.youtube.com/watch?v=-3VOYFupAaw
Art • Look at illustrator's choice of line, colour, texture to create the "shadowy" feel in the illustrations • Look at how photos and drawing have been combined to create illustrations • Create own picture in this style. Could be to illustrate new version of story with different animal	The Learning Challenge CURRICULUM	
Author: Neil Gaiman **Publisher:** Bloomsbury **ISBN:** 0-7475-7472-3		

Planning for Quality Texts: Falling Angels

These documents are intended to support the planning of effective literacy units based on high quality picture books. They are not intended to be lesson plans, but offer a menu of possible ideas for teachers to use as starting points to plan for purposeful learning and give pupils reasons for writing as well as the skills they need to write with impact on their reader. They follow a learning sequence:

- a hook to fully engage and interest the children
- responding to reading activities to allow immersion in and exploration of the text, including picture exploration, book and writer talk
- capturing ideas activities which include drama and talk to support understanding of the text and to develop vocabulary, language and ideas for writing
- possibilities for the contextualised teaching of grammar
- sentence games to develop creativity, vocabulary, language and grammar
- links to guided reading
- a range of writing tasks which may be final unit outcomes or incidental opportunities during the unit

Specific mention is made of the writing sequence:

- modelled writing - teacher models the writing process aloud and the decisions writers make about sentences, paragraphs etc to create impact on the reader. This can also include the modelling of planning and spelling strategies.
- shared writing - collaborative composition with discussion and suggestions about what to write and how to write it to create the intended effect. At this point children may write a sentence/s, often in pairs, on whiteboards which are then discussed.
- guided writing - small group sessions based on specific needs of a specific group of children. The session may address misconceptions, bridge gaps or extend learning and can take place at any point during the unit.

In addition, cross-curricular links are suggested, including links to challenges from the Learning Challenge Curriculum.

YEAR 3,4,5 AND 6

Possible Written Outcomes or Incidental Writing Opportunities
- Diary entry or first person account in role as Sally
- Diary entry in role as grandmother
- Identity card or CV for a character from picture who was in the spotlight
- Narrative - Sally's adventure in one of the places she flies to
- Note/letter to mother persuading her that the adventures are real
- Paragraph to explain "Some people see the world with their eyes. Some people see the world with their hearts."
- Book review to recommend Falling Angels
- If you could fly anywhere, where would you go? Paragraph using speculative and hypothetical language.
- Experimental sentences for poem
- Memory box poem in style of The Magic Box

Hook
- Magic/memory box left out in classroom
- Google earth Flight Simulator

1. Responding to the Text
- Visual Literacy: Use front cover to predict content
- Book talk: Have you any questions about the story? Does it remind you of anything?
- Book talk: do you think that Sally's adventures are real?
- Book talk: why do Sally's grandmother and mother think differently about Sally's stories?
- Visual literacy: look at double page of doors. What might be behind them? Compare with next two pages.
- Book talk: what does the writer mean by saying some people see the world with eyes and some with their hearts?
- Book talk: how does Sally change as she grows up? How do her experiences change how she sees the world?
- Book talk: what are the themes in the book?
- Writer talk: find examples of how the writer structures sentences several clauses. What is the effect?
- Writer talk: how does the writer create images in the readers' head? What language features does he use?

2. Capturing Ideas
- Make story map of events and Sally's travels
- Role on the wall for Sally
- Role play phone call with Sally
- Spotlight characters in detailed pictures and
- Discuss the two ideas of flying and coming down to earth. Do they have more than one meaning? Explain ideas.
- In groups/pairs take one of the places Sally flies to. What adventure might she have had?
- Research location chosen
- Use mapping, story mountain or boxing up to plan an event in one of the places
- Annotate plan with details that will give the reader clues about the setting
- Make own memory box of the precious and interesting things in your life so far
- Explore the poem The Magic Box and the use of figurative language
- Prepare a performance of The Magic Box
- Using the memories from your box, play with building poetic sentences using descriptive and figurative language
- Orally rehearse and revise

Sentence Games (use throughout unit)
- Simile game
- Metaphor game
- Personification game
- Improve a sentence- focus on the grammatical elements that need consolidation or review
- Just a minute game to describe a character from a prop - button, hat, shoe etc or a picture

Guided Reading Possibilities
- Falling Angels or other Colin Thompson books to develop inferential skills and make comparisons
- The Magic Box poem by Kit Wright. Look at use of figurative language and pattern of lines and verses.
- Identify and discuss features of text type for final written outcome. Level of text can be pitched at each groups' level, ensuring both access and challenge.

3. Contextualised Grammar Teaching
- Building effective sentences with several clauses to add information
- Expanded noun phrases to create a picture for the reader
- Use of comma to mark boundaries of clauses

4. Modelled Writing
Shared Writing
Guided Writing
Independent Writing

MAKING LINKS ACROSS THE CURRICULUM

Geography
- Find the places Sally visits on a map and plot her journeys
- Research these locations

DT/ICT
- Develop images for own fantasy world
- Make a partitioned box to hold memories

PSHE
- Falling Angels looks at loss and death. Possibility of discussion around bereavement if appropriate.
- Other useful books on this theme - The Gift by Carol Ann Duffy and Death, Duck and the Tulip by Wolf Erlbruch
-

Useful links
Google Earth
Google Earth Flight Simulator

Art
- Design a door for the lid of the memory box

The Learning Challenge
CURRICULUM

Author: Colin Thompson
Publisher: Random House Australia
ISBN: 978-1-74166-420-1

Planning for Quality Texts: Castles

These documents are intended to support the planning of effective literacy units based on high quality picture books. They are not intended to be lesson plans, but offer a menu of possible ideas for teachers to use as starting points to plan for purposeful learning and give pupils reasons for writing as well as the skills they need to write with impact on their reader. They follow a learning sequence:

- a hook to fully engage and interest the children
- responding to reading activities to allow immersion in and exploration of the text, including picture exploration, book and writer talk
- capturing ideas activities which include drama and talk to support understanding of the text and to develop vocabulary, language and ideas for writing
- possibilities for the contextualised teaching of grammar
- sentence games to develop creativity, vocabulary, language and grammar
- links to guided reading
- a range of writing tasks which may be final unit outcomes or incidental opportunities during the unit

Specific mention is made of the writing sequence:

- modelled writing - teacher models the writing process aloud and the decisions writers make about sentences, paragraphs etc to create impact on the reader. This can also include the modelling of planning and spelling strategies.
- shared writing - collaborative composition with discussion and suggestions about what to write and how to write it to create the intended effect. At this point children may write a sentence/s, often in pairs, on whiteboards which are then discussed.
- guided writing - small group sessions based on specific needs of a specific group of children. The session may address misconceptions, bridge gaps or extend learning and can take place at any point during the unit.

In addition, cross-curricular links are suggested, including links to challenges from the Learning Challenge Curriculum.

YEAR 3,4,5 AND 6

Possible Written Outcomes or Incidental Writing Opportunities

- For sale notice for chosen/invented castle
- Information text for the castle of fire
- Menu for a banquet/afternoon tea at identified castle
- Promotional leaflet/presentation for a day out at chosen castle
- Explanation - Why were castles built?
- Invented castle information for I Spy Guide to Castles
- Wanted poster for character wanting to invade castle
- Character profile for invented character/s
- Narrative based on invented castle and family, using planned structure
- Evaluation of castle made from clay or mouldable material

Hook

- Visit to a castle
- Virtual tour of castle (see useful links)

1. Responding to the Text

- Visual Literacy: spot the royal families living in each castle
- Visual literacy: use different castles in groups and find clues that tell you about the kind of castle it is
- Visual literacy: who might live in the castle?
- Book talk: which is your favourite castle? Is there one you do not like?
- Book talk: why might these castles have been built??
- Book talk: what might be the threat for each castle?
- Writer talk: why is there more text for some castles and less for others?
- Book talk: what stories do you know with castles in them? What genre are they? What are the key features - characters, problem etc
- Box up a story you know or plot it onto a story mountain or flow chart
- Writer talk: what kind of language would you expect to see in these stories? Make a list.

2. Capturing Ideas

- Turn reading area into a castle with storytellers' throne
- Use castle of fire picture and annotate with word bank using nouns, verbs, adverbs, adjectives
- Visualise and sketch an invented castle
- Annotate sketch with word bank as above
- Create a family tree for the royal family living in chosen or invented castle and annotate with characteristics of each person
- Invent a threat for the castle and its family
- Box up or use a story mountain or flow chart to plan a story for your castle - all is well, threat comes along, castle/characters in danger, danger is overcome, all is well
- Develop an opening which describes the castle and its setting
- Develop an ending which returns to opening or comments on events
- Annotate your plan with key narrative language
- Tell your story orally
- Explore sayings about castles - king of the castle, castles in the air, home is my castle
- Debate - "A man's home is his castle"

Sentence Games (use throughout unit)

- Sentence signposts persuasive language game
- Character game - use feelings (anger, fear, cruelty, joy) what would character say to show not tell how they are feeling
- Improve a sentence- focus on the grammatical elements that need consolidation or review
- Sentence starters game from base sentence - focus on fronted adverbials, ing and ed

Guided Reading Possibilities

- Range of traditional stories with castles as settings. Look at structure and use of key narrative language.
- The Princess' Blankets by Carol Ann Duffy. Look at techniques used to develop characterisation - showing not telling
- Identify and discuss features of text type for final written outcome. Level of text can be pitched at each groups' level, ensuring both access and challenge.

3. Contextualised Grammar Teaching

- Use of action and dialogue to show characterisation
- Vary sentence types to build or slow pace
- Choice of verbs to describe actions

4. Modelled Writing
Shared Writing
Guided Writing
Independent Writing

MAKING LINKS ACROSS THE CURRICULUM

Geography/Science
- Materials used for building castles
- Locations and positions of castles

Maths
- Costings for day out at castle

ICT
- Record invented story and add sound effects
- Create online for sale advert for castle
- Design a coat of arms

PSHE
- "A man's home is his castle". What a home represents. Homelessness. Family.

Useful links
http://www.english-heritage.org.uk/daysout/properties/dover-castle/great-tower/virtual-tour/
http://www.youtube.com/watch?v=k6xMK-I_NCo
http://www.youtube.com/watch?v=rx-w5nZwTlk

Art/DT
- Make a castle with clay or other mouldable material
- Use techniques and tools to make and refine castle

Year 4 History:
Why were Norman castles certainly not bouncy?

The Learning Challenge CURRICULUM

Author: Colin Thompson
Publisher: Red Fox
ISBN: 978-0-099-43942-4

Planning with Quality Texts: The Great Kapok Tree

These documents are intended to support the planning of effective literacy units based on high quality picture books. They are not intended to be lesson plans, but offer a menu of possible ideas for teachers to use as starting points to plan for purposeful learning and give pupils reasons for writing as well as the skills they need to write with impact on their reader. They follow a learning sequence:

- a hook to fully engage and interest the children
- responding to reading activities to allow immersion in and exploration of the text, including picture exploration, book and writer talk
- capturing ideas activities which include drama and talk to support understanding of the text and to develop vocabulary, language and ideas for writing
- possibilities for the contextualised teaching of grammar
- sentence games to develop creativity, vocabulary, language and grammar
- links to guided reading
- a range of writing tasks which may be final unit outcomes or incidental opportunities during the unit

Specific mention is made of the writing sequence:

- modelled writing - teacher models the writing process aloud and the decisions writers make about sentences, paragraphs etc to create impact on the reader. This can also include the modelling of planning and spelling strategies.
- shared writing - collaborative composition with discussion and suggestions about what to write and how to write it to create the intended effect. At this point children may write a sentence/s, often in pairs, on whiteboards which are then discussed.
- guided writing - small group sessions based on specific needs of a specific group of children. The session may address misconceptions, bridge gaps or extend learning and can take place at any point during the unit.

In addition, cross-curricular links are suggested, including links to challenges from the Learning Challenge Curriculum.

Possible Written Outcomes or Incidental Writing Opportunities

- Thought bubbles/speech bubbles
- Dialogue between animals
- Fact files/report on rain forest animal/s or rain forest
- Travel agent's leaflet on Brazilian rain forest
- Poster about conservation of rain forest
- Descriptive writing - setting/creatures
- Diary entry/letter to employer explaining why the tree was not cut down
- Re-writing sections of text to further engage the reader
- Newspaper/TV report
- Debate on conservation of rain forest - discussion writing
- Poem based on illustration

KEY STAGE 2

Hook

- Create rainforest environment in classroom
- Create mini-environment outside
- Use rainforest soundscape and play as children enter darkened classroom
- Slide show of devastated rain forest

1. Responding to the Text

- Look at final picture and discuss what might have happened and who the man might be
- **Book talk:** What do you like/dislike about the book? Are there any puzzles or reminders in the book?
- **Picture exploration:** capturing pictures in 3 verbs/adverbs/adjectives
- **Picture exploration:** turn the volume up. What sounds can be heard?
- **Writer talk:** In groups, consider how sentences are started and the impact?
- **Writer talk:** How do the word choices help to paint a picture in our heads? What if there were no illustrations?
- **Writer talk:** Chart all the reasons given by the rain forest creatures. Look at the language they use. Consider the use of persuasive devices - emotive vocabulary, facts, empathy etc. How effective are they?

2. Capturing Ideas

- Role play conversation between creatures before speaking to man
- Developing questions and hot seating characters
- Interview creatures/men
- Develop a range of adverbials (prepositional phrases) to support descriptive writing
- Discuss how the text would need developing if it was not a picture book. Annotate pictures with words/phrases/similes/metaphors as appropriate to year group and learning need
- Drama activity - meeting. Children in role as creatures of the rainforest and teacher as their leader/children as workers and teacher as company owner
- Debate - should we save the rainforest? Identify discursive language required and evaluate its use

Sentence Games (use throughout unit)

- Persuasion game - use persuasive openers to structure oral argument from given scenarios
- Experiment with a range of conjunctions to construct sentences using 2 given nouns. Extend if appropriate with connecting adverbs btween sentences
- Create poetic sentences using listed prepositions - Behind the great tree is the shimmer of afternoon heat, Under the great tree lies a tangle of emerald leaves
- Generate collective nouns - a quivering of tree frogs, a snooze of sloths
- Improve a sentence - focus on the grammatical elements that need consolidation or review

Guided Reading Possibilities

- Non-fiction texts on rainforest/deforestation
- Other rain forest stories - e.g. State of Wonder by Ann Pratchett, The Journey to the River Sea by Eva Ibbotson
- Identify and discuss features of text type for final written outcome. Level of text can be pitched at each groups' level, ensuring both access and challenge.

Contextualised Grammar Teaching

- Use of adverbials as sentence openers
- Use of dialogue and related punctuation and speech tags to show characters' feelings
- Use of connecting adverbs to support the construction and cohesion of discursive writing

4. Modelled Writing
Shared Writing
Guided Writing
Independent Writing

MAKING LINKS ACROSS THE CURRICULUM

Geography
- Links within learning challenge

PSHE
- How do we take responsibility for our own actions? Do we consider the impact of actions on others?

Science
- Life cycle of plants
- Water cycle
- Habitat and adaptation

Art/Music
- Create rain forest environment
- Links within learning challenge
- Create soundscape using instruments

Useful links
- http://my.rainforest-alliance.org
- http://www.rain-tree.com

Year 5 Geography
Why should the rain forest be important to us all?

The Learning Challenge
CURRICULUM

Author: Lynne Cherry
Publisher: Harcourt Books
ISBN: 978-0-15-202614-1

Planning for Quality Texts: Stone Age Boy

These documents are intended to support the planning of effective literacy units based on high quality picture books. They are not intended to be lesson plans, but offer a menu of possible ideas for teachers to use as starting points to plan for purposeful learning and give pupils reasons for writing as well as the skills they need to write with impact on their reader. They follow a learning sequence:

- a hook to fully engage and interest the children
- responding to reading activities to allow immersion in and exploration of the text, including picture exploration, book and writer talk
- capturing ideas activities which include drama and talk to support understanding of the text and to develop vocabulary, language and ideas for writing
- possibilities for the contextualised teaching of grammar
- sentence games to develop creativity, vocabulary, language and grammar
- links to guided reading
- a range of writing tasks which may be final unit outcomes or incidental opportunities during the unit

Specific mention is made of the writing sequence:

- modelled writing - teacher models the writing process aloud and the decisions writers make about sentences, paragraphs etc to create impact on the reader. This can also include the modelling of planning and spelling strategies.
- shared writing - collaborative composition with discussion and suggestions about what to write and how to write it to create the intended effect. At this point children may write a sentence/s, often in pairs, on whiteboards which are then discussed.
- guided writing - small group sessions based on specific needs of a specific group of children. The session may address misconceptions, bridge gaps or extend learning and can take place at any point during the unit.

In addition, cross-curricular links are suggested, including links to challenges from the Learning Challenge Curriculum.

Possible Written Outcomes or Incidental Writing Opportunities

- Speech/thought bubbles for first meeting between the boy and Om
- Use Comic Life to create comic strip of first meeting
- Instructions - How to make tools/How to make fire/How to catch a mammoth
- Day in the life of a Stone Age boy
- Letter home to family in the present day
- Letter to Om after he has returned
- Fact File on aspect of life in the Stone Age
- fact File on an animal found in the Stone Age
- Report on a people of Ancient Britain
- Write more developed text for specific pages - 18, 2/21, 27/28/29
- Explain where would be a good place to live in the Stone Age and why

YEAR 3

Hook

- Spend a lesson with only what would have been available in the Stone Age
- Watch BBC History video - A day in the life of a 10 year old in the Stone Age

1. Responding to the Text

- Visual Literacy: use front cover. What might happen in this book? What clues are there?
- Book talk: do you think this a non-fiction or fiction book? Give reasons.
- Book talk: does the book remind of other stories where the main character goes into another world?
- Role on the wall for the boy
- Book talk: find the clues on pages 12 to 14 that show he is set in the Stone Age
- Visual Literacy: look at page 10. Turn the volume up: what would be heard?
- Writer talk: look closely at the language that adds detail to the text and engages the reader. Find strong verbs, effective adjectives, specific nouns and similes.
- Writer talk: look closely at the sentence starters. Find all the time adverbs and adverbials. How to they help the reader to understand the pace?

2. Capturing Ideas

- Role play first meeting between the boy and Om
- Telephone conversation between boy and family member
- Freeze frame scenes from pages 12 to 15 and thought track. Take photos and add thought bubbles.
- Debate - Would it be fun to be a child in the Stone Age?
- Research life in the Stone Age and the peoples of Ancient Britain. Text mark key information and make notes, highlighting specific vocabulary
- Annotate notes with generalisers and time adverbs/adverbials
- Experiment with forming sentences from notes and annotations
- Use planning format to group related material and decide on sub-headings
- Use illustrations pages 18, 2/21, 27/28/29. Annotate with nouns and adjectives, verbs and adverbs.
- Experiment with forming sentences and consider their effectiveness
- Find out about animals from the Stone Age

Sentence Games (use throughout unit)

- Topic sentence game - give topic sentence. Children suggest contents of paragraph
- Conjunctions game
- Improve a sentence- focus on the grammatical elements that need consolidation or review
- Fortunately, unfortunately game using pictures from book to secure concept of a sentence

Guided Reading Possibilities

- Ug: Boy Genius of the Stone Age by Raymond Briggs
- Non-fiction texts on the Stone Age and Ancient Britain
- Identify and discuss features of text type for final written outcome. Level of text can be pitched at each groups' level, ensuring both access and challenge.

3. Contextualised Grammar Teaching

- Adverbs and adverbials of time to structure chronological writing and increase or slow pace
- Structuring topic sentences to open paragraphs or sections
- Use of co-ordinating and subordinating conjunctions to form informative sentences

4. Modelled Writing
Shared Writing
Guided Writing
Independent Writing

MAKING LINKS ACROSS THE CURRICULUM

Science
- See Science Learning Challenge
- Plan and create stone circle outside. How are the Shadows formed and how and why do they change during the day

History
- See History learning Challenge

DT/ICT
- Design and build a shelter with materials a Stone Age family would have had

Useful links

http://www.bbc.co.uk/history/handsonhistory/ancient-britain.shtml

Art
- Look at cave paintings - subjects, materials and colours used
- Make own paint colours from natural resources. For example - onion skins
- Create cave paintings using natural materials - charcoal, chalk, natural paint colours

Year 3 History:
Who first lived in Britain?
Year 3 Science:
How far can you throw your shadow?

The Learning Challenge CURRICULUM

Author: Satoshi Kitamura
Publisher: Candlewick Press
ISBN: 978-0-7636-3474-2

Planning with Quality Texts: Jamil's Clever Cat

These documents are intended to support the planning of effective literacy units based on high quality picture books. They are not intended to be lesson plans, but offer a menu of possible ideas for teachers to use as starting points to plan for purposeful learning and give pupils reasons for writing as well as the skills they need to write with impact on their reader. They follow a learning sequence:

- a hook to fully engage and interest the children
- responding to reading activities to allow immersion in and exploration of the text, including picture exploration, book and writer talk
- capturing ideas activities which include drama and talk to support understanding of the text and to develop vocabulary, language and ideas for writing
- possibilities for the contextualised teaching of grammar
- sentence games to develop creativity, vocabulary, language and grammar
- links to guided reading
- a range of writing tasks which may be final unit outcomes or incidental opportunities during the unit

Specific mention is made of the writing sequence:

- modelled writing - teacher models the writing process aloud and the decisions writers make about sentences, paragraphs etc to create impact on the reader. This can also include the modelling of planning and spelling strategies.
- shared writing - collaborative composition with discussion and suggestions about what to write and how to write it to create the intended effect. At this point children may write a sentence/s, often in pairs, on whiteboards which are then discussed.
- guided writing - small group sessions based on specific needs of a specific group of children. The session may address misconceptions, bridge gaps or extend learning and can take place at any point during the unit.

In addition, cross-curricular links are suggested, including links to challenges from the Learning Challenge Curriculum.

Possible Written Outcomes or Incidental Writing Opportunities

- Narrative writing/Change the ending
- Write comparison with Puss In Boots
- Adventure Story
- Diary writing
- Instruction writing
- Report writing (Cats)
- Thought/Speech bubbles

YEAR 3

Hook

- Indian clothes/artefacts scattered round room
- Quote: I will make your dream come true

1. Responding to the Text

- Use front cover. Ask questions about where the story might be set
- Picture exploration: Predicting possibilities
- Story map/timeline of events or mapping journey
- Book talk: vivid colours, likes, dislikes, puzzles and reminders
- Writer talk: Discuss use of speech/speech marks?
- Writer talk: How is the text organised?
- Writer talk: What types of sentences have been used? What is the effect?
- Writer talk: Look at word choices

2. Capturing Ideas

- Role play
- Freeze frame role plays at different points
- Hot seat Cat at different points in the story
- Explore Weaver's and Princess' feelings at different points in the story
- Generate when/where/how adverbials and annotate story map/timeline with possibilities
- Watch Report about Cats and identify question types and formal sentence structures for responses
- Role play interviewer/cat expert interview(could be filmed and evaluated)

Sentence Games (use throughout unit)

- Conjunctions game
- Collective nouns
- Warming up the word - generating synonyms for Character' feelings
- Adjectives and adverbs to describe animals and objects in book
- Improve a basic sentence using Fional French techniques
  Chain writing with "Cats" as starting point.

Guided Reading Possibilities

- Read and explore stories from other cultures.
- Other traditional stories/Puss In Boots
- Identify and discuss features of text type for final written outcome. Level of text can be pitched at each groups' level, ensuring both access and challenge.

3. Contextualised Grammar Teaching

- Develop use of speech marks/inverted commas
- Develop expanded noun phrases
- Text is written in the present tense - explore changing to past tense. Investigation into past tense formation
- Use generated adverbials to experiment with creating different effects in sentences

4. Modelled Writing
Shared Writing
Guided Writing
Independent Writing

MAKING LINKS ACROSS THE CURRICULUM

Geography
- Living in Bengal/Asia

Science
- Investigate cat habitat
- Investigate other habitats and consider why they are suitable for particular creatures

Art
- Pattern making using style and colours of illustrations

Useful Links

- http://www.tes.co.uk/teaching-resource/Jamil-and-39-s-Clever-Cat-Book-6260304/

PSHE
- How has the cat helped the weaver?
- What can you do to be helpful?
- What is your dream?
- How can you achieve your dream?

The Learning Challenge
CURRICULUM

Author: Fiona French
Publisher: Francis Lincoln Children's Books
ISBN: 978-1845075187

Planning for Quality Texts: Fly, Eagle, Fly!

These documents are intended to support the planning of effective literacy units based on high quality books. They are not intended to be lesson plans, but offer a menu of possible ideas for teachers to use as starting points to plan for purposeful learning and give pupils reasons for writing as well as the skills they need to write with impact on their reader. They follow a learning sequence:

- a hook to fully engage and interest the children
- responding to reading activities to allow immersion in and exploration of the text, including picture exploration, book and writer talk
- capturing ideas activities which include drama and talk to support understanding of the text and to develop vocabulary, language and ideas for writing
- possibilities for the contextualised teaching of grammar
- sentence games to develop creativity, vocabulary, language and grammar
- links to guided reading
- a range of writing tasks which may be final unit outcomes or incidental opportunities during the unit

Specific mention is made of the writing sequence:

- modelled writing - teacher models the writing process aloud and the decisions writers make about sentences, paragraphs etc to create impact on the reader. This can also include the modelling of planning and spelling strategies.
- shared writing - collaborative composition with discussion and suggestions about what to write and how to write it to create the intended effect. At this point children may write a sentence/s, often in pairs, on whiteboards which are then discussed.
- guided writing - small group sessions based on specific needs of a specific group of children. The session may address misconceptions, bridge gaps or extend learning and can take place at any point during the unit.

In addition, cross-curricular links are suggested, including links to challenges from the Learning Challenge Curriculum.

Possible Written Outcomes or Incidental Writing Opportunities

- Write in role as the farmer when he finds the eagle chick, when he is trying to make it behave like a chicken and when he releases the eagle
- Write in role as the farmer's friend making the point of view clear
- Write in role as the eagle trying to persuade the farmer that he is not a chicken
- Write from the eagle's point of view following his release
- Message from the eagle to the farmer's friend thanking him
- Retell the story incorporating fronted adverbials to link ideas between paragraphs
- Aspirational message for class display
- Information text about eagles
- Create a list poem about an eagle

YEAR 3 AND 4

Hook

- Footage of eagle in flight
- Key picture activity - see responding to text
- Visit to see birds of prey

1. Responding to the Text

- Visual literacy: Choose some key pictures from the book. Give one to each pair/group. Annotate pictures with ideas about what could be happening. Pairs/groups work to order pictures and predict storyline.
- Book talk: Read text and compare with picture sequence and initial ideas.
- Book talk: What clues are there that show that this is set in another time and culture?
- Book talk: What might be the main theme? What does the writer want us to understand?
- Book talk: Why do you think the farmer wants the eagle to be a chicken?
- Book talk: How do you think the eagle feels? Did he really think he was a chicken? How does he feel when the farmer's friend is trying to make him fly?
- Book talk: Read the foreword by Desmond Tutu. How does this help us to understand the story and its theme
- Writer talk: Explore the unfamiliar vocabulary and meanings
- Writer talk: How does the writer make links between events and paragraphs?

2. Capturing Ideas

- Freeze frame and thought track different scenes
- Make a story map
- Retell story orally from story map
- Add adverbials to the map to support making links between paragraphs and incorporate in retell
- Think of questions to ask the eagle
- Hot seat the eagle
- Role on the wall for the eagle - how did he behave/how did he feel inside?
- Role play the eagle trying to persuade the farmer that he is not a chicken
- Debate - Can an eagle ever be a chicken? (Can the way we are treated influence what we want to be?)
- Discuss hopes and aspirations for the future. Model modal language. Present their aspirations formally using modelled language
- Research eagles, including photographs and paintings
- Develop descriptive language - verbs, adverbs, adjectives and adjectival phrases

Sentence Games (use throughout unit)

- Messing about with modals game
- Preposition game
- Sentence starter game - focus on fronted adverbials
- Persuasion game

Guided Reading Possibilities

- Read other stories set in Africa - Mufaro's Beautiful Daughters, The Village that Vanished.
- Explore the poem The Eagle by Alfred, Lord Tennyson
- Identify and discuss features of text type for final written outcome. Level of text can be pitched at each groups' level, ensuring both access and challenge.

3. Contextualised Grammar Teaching

- Prepositions and prepositional phrases
- Fronted adverbials

4. Modelled Writing
Shared Writing
Guided Writing
Independent Writing

MAKING LINKS ACROSS THE CURRICULUM

Geography/Science/History
- Geographical, physical features of African countries
- Habitats and characteristics of mammals
-

Maths

ICT
- Find paintings and photos of eagles and create digital montage

PSHE
- Have they ever felt like the eagle in the story?
- Should we try to influence anyone or thing to be something it was not intended to be?

Useful links
http://www.poemhunter.com/poem/the-eagle-2/

Art/DT
- Observational drawings of eagles
- Looking at patterns created by feathers, sketching and creating own

The Learning Challenge
CURRICULUM

Author: Christopher Gregowski
Publisher: Frances Lincoln
ISBN: 0780711217300

Planning for Quality Texts: Escape From Pompeii

These documents are intended to support the planning of effective literacy units based on high quality picture books. They are not intended to be lesson plans, but offer a menu of possible ideas for teachers to use as starting points to plan for purposeful learning and give pupils reasons for writing as well as the skills they need to write with impact on their reader. They follow a learning sequence:

- a hook to fully engage and interest the children
- responding to reading activities to allow immersion in and exploration of the text, including picture exploration, book and writer talk
- capturing ideas activities which include drama and talk to support understanding of the text and to develop vocabulary, language and ideas for writing
- possibilities for the contextualised teaching of grammar
- sentence games to develop creativity, vocabulary, language and grammar
- links to guided reading
- a range of writing tasks which may be final unit outcomes or incidental opportunities during the unit

Specific mention is made of the writing sequence:

- modelled writing - teacher models the writing process aloud and the decisions writers make about sentences, paragraphs etc. to create impact on the reader. This can also include the modelling of planning and spelling strategies.
- shared writing - collaborative composition with discussion and suggestions about what to write and how to write it to create the intended effect. At this point children may write a sentence/s, often in pairs, on whiteboards which are then discussed.
- guided writing - small group sessions based on specific needs of a specific group of children. The session may address misconceptions, bridge gaps or extend learning and can take place at any point during the unit.

In addition, cross-curricular links are suggested, including links to challenges from the Learning Challenge Curriculum.

YEAR 3 AND 4

Possible Written Outcomes or Incidental Writing Opportunities

- Diary entry in role as Tranio or Livia on the day after the eruption
- Letter to relative in Britain describing events
- Explanation - volcanic eruption
- Fact file on earthquakes and volcanoes
- Non-chronological report on daily life in Pompeii
- Thought bubbles of city dwellers before and during eruption
- Evacuation instructions
- Using picture of volcano erupting, description of eruption
- Eye-witness account
- Discussion/comparative report - Should people re-build towns and cities close to active volcanoes?
- For sale notice for home in Pompeii
- Volcano poem

Hook

- Enter darkened classroom with video of volcanic eruption in progress
- Roman day in school

1. Responding to the Text

- Book talk: how is the plot structured? What is the climax of the story?
- Book talk: how does the writer build up towards the climax?
- Visual literacy: how do the illustrations help us to understand how the people felt?
- Book talk: why does the writer include the poet's song near the beginning of the book? What impact does this have on the reader?
- Book talk: find clues in the text and the illustrations which tell the reader the book is set in Roman times and in another place
- Book talk: why has the writer included information at the back of the book? Is this a fiction or non-fiction book?
- Make story map/timeline of events
- Writer talk: how does the writer add pace to the events? Look at choice of verbs and structure of sentences.

2. Capturing Ideas

- Text mark key information that gives detail about everyday life in Pompeii
- Note additional information about everyday life found in illustrations
- Research earthquakes and volcanic eruptions, text mark key information and make notes, highlighting technical vocabulary
- Annotate notes with generalisers and adverbs of cause and effect
- Experiment with forming sentences from notes and annotations
- Research towns and cities which have been re-built close to active volcanoes, listing advantages and disadvantages
- Debate in role as townspeople who want to re-build and those who are against it
- Freeze frame and thought track different scenes in the city before and during eruption
- Interview survivors
- Build word bank of nouns, verbs, adverbs and adjectives to describe eruption
- Loudspeaker broadcast to warn the people of Pompeii

Sentence Games (use throughout unit)

- Topic sentence game - give topic sentence. Children suggest contents of paragraph
- Metaphor game
- Conjunction game
- Improve a sentence- focus on the grammatical elements that need consolidation or review

Guided Reading Possibilities

- Non-fiction texts on volcanoes and earthquakes
- Non-fiction texts on the Romans
- Atlantis: Legend of a Lost City by Christina Balit. Find clues relating to context.
- Identify and discuss features of text type for final written outcome. Level of text can be pitched at each groups' level, ensuring both access and challenge.

3. Contextualised Grammar Teaching

- Fronted adverbials to describe an event
- Choice of verbs to convey pace
- Look at simile and metaphor and develop a range from word bank created
- Develop poetic sentences with a focus on starting them in different ways - adverbials, ing, ed, simile
- Connecting adverbs of cause and effect

4. Modelled Writing
Shared Writing
Guided Writing
Independent Writing

MAKING LINKS ACROSS THE CURRICULUM

Geography/Science	History	ICT
• See Year 3 Geography Learning Challenge • See Year 3 Science Learning Challenge: What do rocks tell us about the way the earth was formed?	• See Year 4 History Learning Challenge	• Use images in a slide-show/animoto to support explanation of how volcanoes erupt • Add sound to slide-show
DT • Make a game like "knucklebones" and write instructions for it		**Useful links** http://museumvictoria.com.au/education/learning-lab/ancient-roman-empire/recreation-of-vesuvius-erupting/
Art • Create repeating patterns in the style of the edges of pages in text, choosing colour and tones appropriately	**Year 3 Geography: What makes the earth angry? Year 4 History: Why were the Romans so powerful and what did we learn from them?** The Learning Challenge CURRICULUM	
Author: Christina Balit **Publisher:** Francis Lincoln **ISBN:** 978-1-84507-059-5		

Planning for Quality Texts: The Fox and the Star

These documents are intended to support the planning of effective literacy units based on high quality books. They are not intended to be lesson plans, but offer a menu of possible ideas for teachers to use as Starting points to plan for purposeful learning and give pupils reasons for writing as well as the skills they need to write with impact on their reader. They follow a learning sequence:

- a hook to fully engage and interest the children
- responding to reading activities to allow immersion in and exploration of the text, including picture exploration, book and writer talk
- capturing ideas activities which include drama and talk to support understanding of the text and to develop vocabulary, language and ideas for writing
- possibilities for the contextualised teaching of grammar
- sentence games to develop creativity, vocabulary, language and grammar
- links to guided reading
- a range of writing tasks which may be final unit outcomes or incidental opportunities during the unit

Specific mention is made of the writing sequence:

- modelled writing - teacher models the writing process aloud and the decisions writers make about sentences, paragraphs etc. to create impact on the reader. This can also include the modelling of planning and spelling strategies.
- shared writing - collaborative composition with discussion and suggestions about what to write and how to write it to create the intended effect. At this point children may write a sentence/s, often in pairs, on whiteboards which are then discussed.
- guided writing - small group sessions based on specific needs of a specific group of children. The session may address misconceptions, bridge gaps or extend learning and can take place at any point during the unit.

In addition, cross-curricular links are suggested, including links to challenges from the Learning Challenge Curriculum.

Possible Written Outcomes or Incidental Writing Opportunities

- Writing in role
- Thought bubbles
- Speech bubbles into dialogue
- Retell story from a different point of view
- List poem based on forest
- Information text on Fox or other animals or plants
- Glossary of vocabulary
- Before and after the change diary entry in role as Fox
- Further diary entry from the end of the book
- Predict what might happen once Fox leaves the forest
- Information texts on foxes or other animals or plants
- Explain how shadows are formed

YEAR 3 AND 4

Hook

- Show clip of Foxes

https://www.youtube.com/watch?v=sWbdY5p9mTg&index=4&list=PL9SLkANZIEtU_MWrOu0B57hc0MONo0mNM

- Visit to Planetarium

1. Responding to the Text

Book talk: Read the first 4 pages. What do you know about Foxes? How does the writer describe the Fox? What impression does this give of the Fox?
Book talk: How is the Star described? What effect does the Star have on Fox?
Book talk: How do the illustrations tell the reader about the Fox and his relationship with the beetles and the rabbits?
Book talk: Why does the writer include the double page illustration of the Fox's eyes? (Link to text on previous page)
Book talk: Explore next 2 double pages. Why has the text been presented differently? How have the illustrations changed? What effect might this have on Fox? Is the change good?
Book talk: Explore next double page. What is Fox feeling and why? How do you know?
Writer talk: How does the writer use language to show that Fox's feelings are changing?
Book talk: What do you think "Look up beyond your ears" means?
Writer talk: How does the writer use the illustrations to deepen understanding? How do they show Fox's emotions and how he changes?

2. Capturing Ideas

- Collect words and language that writer uses to describe the Fox to begin role on the wall for Fox
- Add to role on wall as book is explored
- Role play conversation between Star and Fox
- Gather feelings vocabulary
- Fortune graph annotated with events and Fox's feelings
- Hot seating of Fox
- Conscience alley – should Fox continue his search after he falls asleep?
- Collect examples of sequential language from text and categorise – how, when, where
- Annotation of illustration with nouns, adjectives, prepositional phrases, ing, ed starters for list poem
- Research Foxes and make notes
- Research other animals or plants and make notes

Sentence Games (use throughout unit)

- Sentence starter game – fronted adverbials
- Sentence starter game – ing and ed starters
- Adverbials sorting game
- Determiners game
- Conjunctions game to join information or explain

Guided Reading Possibilities

- The Fox and the Star
- The Worm and the Bird – Coralie Bickford-Smith
- The Star Tree – Catherine Hyde
- Information books on foxes/animals/plants

3. Contextualised Grammar Teaching

- Use of verbs to show and not tell emotions
- Use of direct speech
- Precise word choices – clines for emotions vocabulary and expanded noun phrases for list poem
- Adverbials to signal changes

4. Modelled Writing
Shared Writing
Guided Writing
Independent Writing

MAKING LINKS ACROSS THE CURRICULUM

Geography/Science/History

- Light sources and shadows
- Identify and name a variety of living things (plants and animals) in the local and wider environment and group them

Art/DT

- Explore the art of William Morris. https://www.william-morris.co.uk/search/?SelectedProductGroups=142
- https://www.william-morris.co.uk/search/?SelectedProductGroups=138
- Design patterns for printing of natural environments

ICT

Music/PE

Useful links

https://www.youtube.com/watch?v=sWbdY5p9mTg&index=4&list=PL9SLkANZIEtU_MWrOu0B57hc0MONo0mNM

Maths

Year 3 Science: How far can you throw your shadow?
Year 4 Science:
Which plants and animals thrive in your locality?

The Learning Challenge
CURRICULUM

Author: Coralie Bickford-Smith
Publisher: Penguin Books
ISBN: 978-0-141-97889-5

Planning for Quality Texts: The Worst Witch

These documents are intended to support the planning of effective literacy units based on high quality books. They are not intended to be lesson plans, but offer a menu of possible ideas for teachers to use as starting points to plan for purposeful learning and give pupils reasons for writing as well as the skills they need to write with impact on their reader. They follow a learning sequence:

- a hook to fully engage and interest the children
- responding to reading activities to allow immersion in and exploration of the text, including picture exploration, book and writer talk
- capturing ideas activities which include drama and talk to support understanding of the text and to develop vocabulary, language and ideas for writing
- possibilities for the contextualised teaching of grammar
- sentence games to develop creativity, vocabulary, language and grammar
- links to guided reading
- a range of writing tasks which may be final unit outcomes or incidental opportunities during the unit

Specific mention is made of the writing sequence:

- modelled writing - teacher models the writing process aloud and the decisions writers make about sentences, paragraphs etc. to create impact on the reader. This can also include the modelling of planning and spelling strategies.
- shared writing - collaborative composition with discussion and suggestions about what to write and how to write it to create the intended effect. At this point children may write a sentence/s, often in pairs, on whiteboards which are then discussed.
- guided writing - small group sessions based on specific needs of a specific group of children. The session may address misconceptions, bridge gaps or extend learning and can take place at any point during the unit.

In addition, cross-curricular links are suggested, including links to challenges from the Learning Challenge Curriculum.

Possible Written Outcomes or Incidental Writing Opportunities

- Writing in role – as Mildred or Ethel at identified points
- Character profiles
- Thought bubbles
- Speech bubbles into dialogue – Mildred and Miss Hardbroom after the display
- Write a recipe for a potion
- Describe making of potion and the result
- Instructions – How to ride a broomstick
- Explanation – linked to science
- Glossary of vocabulary
- Summaries of chapters
- Advert for the Academy
- Letter from Mildred saying why she has decided to run away

YEAR 3 AND 4

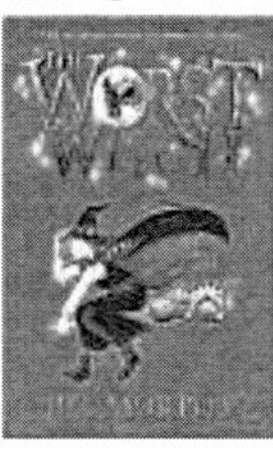

Hook

- Potion making equipment and containers on display

1. Responding to the Text

Book talk: What is your impression of Mildred from Ch 1?
Book talk: Why is the cat so important? Why do Mildred's feelings change about the kitten?
Book talk: Why are Miss Hardbroom's feelings different towards Mildred and Ethel? How do you know?
Book talk: In Ch 4 what do you think will happen when Mildred and Maud taste the potion? How might Miss Hardbroom react?
Book talk: Do you think Miss Cackle is a good headteacher? Explain your ideas.
Book talk: In Ch 5 why does Ethel do something to the broom? Predict what may happen.
Writer talk: Why do you think the writer includes a picture of the chief wizard at the end of Ch6? What is the effect on the reader?
Book talk: Why do you think Mildred decided to run away? Do you think she was right?
Writer talk: How does the writer build tension in Ch8?
Book talk: Why does Miss Cackle believe Mildred about the witches?
Book talk: Do you think Ethel got what she deserved at the end of the book? Explain your ideas.
Book talk: What is your opinion of Miss Hardbroom now?

2. Capturing Ideas

- Role on the wall for Mildred – add to this as book is read
- Role on the wall for Miss Hardbroom – add to this as the book is read
- Visualise and draw Academy from Ch1 description
- Role play conversation between Mildred and Miss Hardbroom after the display
- Fortune graph for Mildred for identified chapter of whole text
- Hot seating of characters – Mildred/Ethel/Miss Hardbroom/Miss Cackle
- Conscience alley – should Mildred run away?
- Develop ideas for potion – ingredients, amount, how they react when mixed, purpose of potion
- Develop sentence starters to narrate the making and impact of the potion

Sentence Games (use throughout unit)

- Sentence starter game – fronted adverbials
- Sentence starter game – ing and ed starters
- Apostrophes – Mildred's, the witches' etc
- Determiners game

Guided Reading Possibilities

- The Worst Witch
- Other books from The Worst Witch Series
- Witches' spell from Macbeth

3. Contextualised Grammar Teaching

- Use of direct speech
- Precise word choices – expanded noun phrases for potion
- Use of first and third person
- Adverbs, conjunctions and prepositions to sequence events

4. Modelled Writing
Shared Writing
Guided Writing
Independent Writing

MAKING LINKS ACROSS THE CURRICULUM

Geography/Science/History

- Forces and magnets
- States of matter

Art/DT

- Design a bottle or container for potion

ICT

Music/PE

Useful links

https://www.bbc.co.uk/education/clips/zm78q6f

Maths

- Measuring ingredients for potion
- Scaling up recipe for different numbers

Year 3 Science:
Are you attractive enough?
Year 4 Science:
How could we survive without water?

The Learning Challenge
CURRICULUM

Author: Jill Murphy
Publisher: Puffin Books
ISBN: 978-0141349596

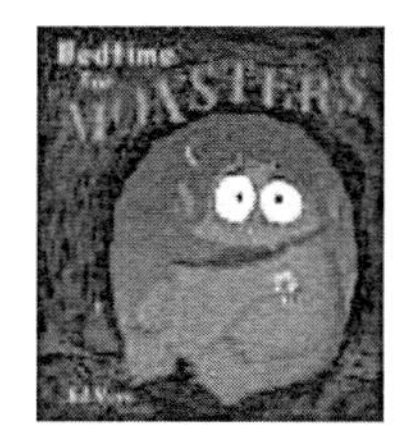

Planning for Quality Texts: Bedtime for Monsters

These documents are intended to support the planning of effective literacy units based on high quality books. They are not intended to be lesson plans, but offer a menu of possible ideas for teachers to use as starting points to plan for purposeful learning and give pupils reasons for writing as well as the skills they need to write with impact on their reader. They follow a learning sequence:

- a hook to fully engage and interest the children
- responding to reading activities to allow immersion in and exploration of the text, including picture exploration, book and writer talk
- capturing ideas activities which include drama and talk to support understanding of the text and to develop vocabulary, language and ideas for writing
- activities focused on the development of spoken language and vocabulary development
- sentence games to develop creativity and the understanding of the concept of a sentence
- links to guided reading
- a range of writing tasks which may be guided in a focus group or incidental opportunities both in and outside the classroom

Specific mention is made of the writing sequence:

- modelled writing - teacher models the writing process aloud and the decisions writers make about sentences and word choices to create impact on the reader. This can also include the modelling of oral rehearsal of sentences and application of phonic learning.
- shared writing - collaborative composition with discussion and suggestions about what to write and how to write it to create the intended effect. At this point children may write a sentence/s, often in pairs, on whiteboards which are then discussed.
- guided writing - small group sessions based on specific needs of a specific group of children. The session may address misconceptions, bridge gaps or extend learning and can take place at any point during the unit.

In addition, cross-curricular links are suggested, including links to challenges from the Learning Challenge Curriculum.

Possible Written/Spoken Outcomes or Incidental Writing/Speaking Opportunities

- Retell story from different point of view
- Write 2 versions – the story the pictures tell, the story beyond the pictures
- Writing in role
- Thought bubbles
- Speech bubbles into direct speech
- Retell story with more detail – description and dialogue
- Character profile
- Develop an additional event for the book both pictures and text
- Explain how the illustrations in a book can tell a different story from the text
- Information writing on living things and their habitats

YEAR 3 AND 4

Hook

- Monster footprints across the room for children to speculate about what might have left them and draw and label character from first thoughts

Responding to the Text

- Book talk: Prediction - Use picture from front cover without title. Who is this? What clues are there? What do you think it is thinking about?
- Book talk: Use p2/3 spread. What can you find out about the setting? Discuss where and how the monsters are positioned, the reasons for dividing the page and the differences in the setting features in each half. Why do you think the monster is in the cave?
- Book talk: Does this remind you of other stories or films?
- Book talk: Share images without text and discuss events and character
- Book talk: Share text and discuss events and character
- Book talk: Were you surprised by the ending? Why/not?
- Book talk: Discuss points of view: the narrator's and the monster's
- Book talk: Is there anything in the illustrations that shows the same point of view as the narrator?
- Writer talk: What techniques does the writer/illustrator use to keep the reader engaged?

2. Capturing Ideas

- Role play interactions to develop dialogue
- Story map journey
- Hot seat monster
- Role on the wall for monster
- Word banks of noun phrases with precise word choices
- Additional settings for new event
- Illustration annotation
- Retell story from different points of view
- Annotate map with sequential fronted adverbials to mark off paragraphs
- Explore use of font and calligrams and develop own for chosen words

Sentence Games (use throughout unit)

- Preposition game
- Sentence starter game - focus on fronted adverbials
- Determiners game

Guided Reading Possibilities

- Other Ed Vere books – Max the Brave, Banana
- Other picture books where the illustrations tell a different story from the text – Rosie's Walk, Not Now, Bernard
- Information texts on plants and animals

Contextualised Grammar

- Expanded noun phrases-expansion before and after the noun, including similes, to describe monster and or settings
- Prepositional phrases, fronted adverbials for setting description
- Inverted commas for dialogue
- Fronted adverbials to sequence events

Modelled Writing
Shared Writing
Guided Writing
Independent Writing

MAKING LINKS ACROSS THE CURRICULUM

History/Geography/Science
- Identify and name a variety of living things (plants and animals) in the local and wider environment and group them

Maths

ICT

Art/DT/Music
- Explore how artists portray and position characters in portraits – Look! Body language in Art by Gillian Wolfe
- https://www.nationalgallery.org.uk/learning/teachers-and-schools/teaching-english-and-drama/how-to-read-a-painting
- Explore the music that Ed Vere used as an ispiration while crafting the book http://www.youtube.com/watch?v=a1AE_bCoPSI
- Develop spread for additional event - http://blog.picturebookmakers.com/post/116986873251/viviane-schwarz

Useful links
https://www.youtube.com/watch?v=5JdAh8OOMVs
https://www.youtube.com/watch?v=vMOLjKAugyA
https://www.youtube.com/watch?v=2OAwz0A0Z6w
http://www.edvere.com/

PSHE
- Making links with own experiences - does the monster want the same things at bedtime as we do?
- Are you afraid of anything at night? What makes you feel safe?

Year 4 Science: Which plants and anlmals survive in your locality?

The Learning Challenge CURRICULUM

Author: Ed Vere
Publisher: Puffin Books
ISBN: 978-0141502397

Planning for Quality Texts: Shh! We Have a Plan

These documents are intended to support the planning of effective literacy units based on high quality books. They are not intended to be lesson plans, but offer a menu of possible ideas for teachers to use as Starting points to plan for purposeful learning and give pupils reasons for writing as well as the skills they need to write with impact on their reader. They follow a learning sequence:

- a hook to fully engage and interest the children
- responding to reading activities to allow immersion in and exploration of the text, including picture exploration, book and writer talk
- capturing ideas activities which include drama and talk to support understanding of the text and to develop vocabulary, language and ideas for writing
- possibilities for the contextualised teaching of grammar
- sentence games to develop creativity, vocabulary, language and grammar
- links to guided reading
- a range of writing tasks which may be final unit outcomes or incidental opportunities during the unit

Specific mention is made of the writing sequence:

- modelled writing - teacher models the writing process aloud and the decisions writers make about sentences, paragraphs etc. to create impact on the reader. This can also include the modelling of planning and spelling strategies.
- shared writing - collaborative composition with discussion and suggestions about what to write and how to write it to create the intended effect. At this point children may write a sentence/s, often in pairs, on whiteboards which are then discussed.
- guided writing - small group sessions based on specific needs of a specific group of children. The session may address misconceptions, bridge gaps or extend learning and can take place at any point during the unit.

In addition, cross-curricular links are suggested, including links to challenges from the Learning Challenge Curriculum.

Possible Written Outcomes or Incidental Writing Opportunities

- Writing in role as one of the three characters
- Writing in role as the small character
- Writing in role as the bird
- Predictions
- Thought bubbles
- Speech bubbles into dialogue
- Retell story from the point of view of a third person narrator
- Instructions – How to look after birds
- Write the characters' plan
- Plan the events of the next chapter and produce illustrations
- Write the text for the illustrations – either in the style of the writer or with more developed text
- Information writing on birds
- Explanation – how shadows are formed

YEAR 3 AND 4

Hook

- Show Laurel and Hardy clip
  Laurel and Hardy: Washing Up
  http://www.youtube.com/watch?v=t_LXd66-zKU

Responding to the Text

Book talk: What might the plan be? What might the characters do? What clues do the illustrations give you?
Book talk: Explore pages to characters in tree about to net bird. Do you think the plan will work?
Book talk: Explore up to LOOK! down there Predict what could happen?
Book talk: Why do you think the writer included the small character? What do you think his relationship is to the others? What do you think he is interested in?
Book talk: What do you think of the ending? Explain your ideas.
Book talk: What does the use of block colour suggest about the story, characters and settings?
Book talk: How do you think the pictures are made? Do they remind you of any other picture books?
Book talk: What is telling more of the story? What difference does it make that there are not many words?
Book talk: How does the writer create humour?
Book talk: What message does the book have? What does the writer want you to feel?
Book talk: There is a pattern of three in the book. Do you know other stories with this pattern?

2. Capturing Ideas

- Role play different scenes
- Freeze frame and thought track different scenes
- Emotions graph for small character
- Role play what might happen after the page LOOK! down there
- Annotate pages with thoughts/speech of characters
- Annotate pages
- Explore techniques used in picture books/film – zoom, wide angle, change of perspective, change of setting
- Find examples in book
- Research birds and make notes
- Research other animals or plants and make notes

Sentence Games (use throughout unit)

- Sentence starter game – fronted adverbials
- Sentence starter game – ing and ed starters
- Adverbials sorting game
- Determiners game
- Conjunctions game to join information or explain

Guided Reading Possibilities

- Shh! We Have a Plan
- Other Chris Haughton books
- Silent films
- Information books on birds/animals/plants

3. Contextualised Grammar Teaching

- Explore use of punctuation (or lack of) in the book
- Identify where dialogue is used and add punctuation
- Develop use of direct speech
- Precise word choices – clines for emotions vocabulary and expanded noun phrases for list poem
- Adverbials to signal changes

4. Modelled Writing
Shared Writing
Guided Writing
Independent Writing

MAKING LINKS ACROSS THE CURRICULUM

Geography/Science/History
- Light sources and shadows
- Identify and name a variety of living things (plants and animals) in the local and wider environment and group them

Art/DT
- Collage work in the style of the book
- Use of colour to create effects

ICT
Laurel and Hardy: Washing Up
http://www.youtube.com/watch?v=t_LXd66-zKU
Buster Keaton: Elevator Chase:
https://www.youtube.com/watch?v=JzZYZj0i3Og
- Make picture book trailer

Music/PE
- Use of music in silent films

Useful links
http://blog.chrishaughton.com/the-making-of-shh-we-have-a-plan/
http://blog.chrishaughton.com/the-making-of-shh-we-have-a-plan/

Maths

Year 3 Science:
How far can you throw your shadow?
Year 4 Science:
Which plants and animals thrive in your locality?

The Learning Challenge
CURRICULUM

Author: Chris Haughton
Publisher: Walker Books
ISBN: 978-1-4063-6003-5

Planning for Quality Texts: The Journey Home

These documents are intended to support the planning of effective literacy units based on high quality books. They are not intended to be lesson plans, but offer a menu of possible ideas for teachers to use as starting points to plan for purposeful learning and give pupils reasons for writing as well as the skills they need to write with impact on their reader. They follow a learning sequence:

- a hook to fully engage and interest the children
- responding to reading activities to allow immersion in and exploration of the text, including picture exploration, book and writer talk
- capturing ideas activities which include drama and talk to support understanding of the text and to develop vocabulary, language and ideas for writing
- possibilities for the contextualised teaching of grammar
- sentence games to develop creativity, vocabulary, language and grammar
- links to guided reading
- a range of writing tasks which may be final unit outcomes or incidental opportunities during the unit

Specific mention is made of the writing sequence:

- modelled writing - teacher models the writing process aloud and the decisions writers make about sentences, paragraphs etc. to create impact on the reader. This can also include the modelling of planning and spelling strategies.
- shared writing - collaborative composition with discussion and suggestions about what to write and how to write it to create the intended effect. At this point children may write a sentence/s, often in pairs, on whiteboards which are then discussed.
- guided writing - small group sessions based on specific needs of a specific group of children. The session may address misconceptions, bridge gaps or extend learning and can take place at any point during the unit.

In addition, cross-curricular links are suggested, including links to challenges from the Learning Challenge Curriculum.

Possible Written Outcomes or Incidental Writing Opportunities

- Thought bubbles and feelings bubbles
- Speech bubbles into direct speech
- Prequel of story
- Next chapter in story
- Fact file/non-chronological report on endangered animal
- Dodo's story
- Add another animal to story following model in book
- Dialogue between animals
- Ship's log in role as polar bear or other animal
- Description of storm
- Setting description of island home
- Writing in role as the animals
- Non-chronological reports including facts about the different animals
- Write – What does tomorrow bring
- Poster to save endangered animal

YEAR 3 AND 4

Hook

- Clips of endangered animals/destroyed environments
- Play Earth Song

Responding to the Text

Book talk: What do you think happened to the bear? How did he get there? What happened before this story started?
Book talk: What impression does the writer give of the city "where machines rumbled and tall buildings hid the sky"?
Book talk: What is the panda thinking and feeling? What do we know about panda? What do you think has happened to the panda? Why is he there?
Book talk: Where are they when they find the orang-utang? What is the setting? What do you think they are thinking? What do you think will happen next?
Book talk: Does the elephant go with the others because his home has been destroyed? How do you know?
Book talk: Do you think it was helpful to the animals that they had been carried far away?
Book talk: Why do you think the writer chose to include a dodo at the end of the book?
Book talk: What do you think the writer means by "Let's see what tomorrow brings."?
Book talk: What do you think the message is for the reader?
Writer talk: Why do you think when the animals sail away, the illustration is round and the text round the illustration?
Writer talk: How do the illustrations help to tell the story and make the message clear?

2. Capturing Ideas

- Story map of key events
- Freeze frame meetings and though track each animal
- Develop bank of emotions vocabulary
- Annotate storm picture – nouns, adjectives, verbs, prepositional phrases
- Role play animals during storm to develop show and not tell language
- Retell an event in role as one of the animals
- Research endangered animals and the reasons why they are endangered
- Role play meetings between bear and chosen animal
- Gather ideas for what could happen next
- Collect examples of persuasive techniques from posters

Sentence Games (use throughout unit)

- Conjunctions game
- Cline activities to explore meaning of emotions vocabulary and rank in intensity
- Change the mood game
- Determiner game

Guided Reading Possibilities

- The Journey Home
- The Dodo – Hilaire Belloc
- Non-fiction material on endangered animals
- Posters and persuasive material to save endangered animals

3. Contextualised Grammar Teaching

- Conjunctions to add information, join similar information and give reasons
- Direct speech
- Show and not tell language to show emotion
- Persuasive techniques for posters

4. Modelled Writing
Shared Writing
Guided Writing
Independent Writing

MAKING LINKS ACROSS THE CURRICULUM

Geography/Science/History	Maths	ICT
• Identify and name a variety of living things (plants and animals) in the local and wider environment and group them • Recognise that environments can change and can pose dangers • Settlements, land use, economic activity including natural resources especially water supplies	• Directional vocabulary and map work related to the story • Co-ordinates to look at the key places from the story • Data handling – different species and numbers	• Data presentation
PSHE • Importance of caring for the environment – conservation matters, global issues, respecting animals		**Useful links** http://news.bbc.co.uk/cbbcnews/hi/find_out/guides/animals/endangered_animals_world/newsid_1614000/1614414.stm https://www.bbc.co.uk/education/clips/zgcmfrd https://www.wwf.org.uk/
Art/DT • Artist studies of animal paintings	**Year 3 Science:** **How did that blossom become an apple?** **Year 4 Science:** **Which animals and plants thrive in your locality?** **Year 4 Geography:** **Where would you choose to build a city?**	The Learning Challenge CURRICULUM
Author: Fran Preston-Gannon **Publisher:** Pavilion Children's Books **ISBN:** 978-1-84365-209-0		

Planning for Quality Texts: Arthur and the Golden Rope

These documents are intended to support the planning of effective literacy units based on high quality books. They are not intended to be lesson plans, but offer a menu of possible ideas for teachers to use as Starting points to plan for purposeful learning and give pupils reasons for writing as well as the skills they need to write with impact on their reader. They follow a learning sequence:

- a hook to fully engage and interest the children
- responding to reading activities to allow immersion in and exploration of the text, including picture exploration, book and writer talk
- capturing ideas activities which include drama and talk to support understanding of the text and to develop vocabulary, language and ideas for writing
- possibilities for the contextualised teaching of grammar
- sentence games to develop creativity, vocabulary, language and grammar
- links to guided reading
- a range of writing tasks which may be final unit outcomes or incidental opportunities during the unit

Specific mention is made of the writing sequence:

- modelled writing - teacher models the writing process aloud and the decisions writers make about sentences, paragraphs etc. to create impact on the reader. This can also include the modelling of planning and spelling strategies.
- shared writing - collaborative composition with discussion and suggestions about what to write and how to write it to create the intended effect. At this point children may write a sentence/s, often in pairs, on whiteboards which are then discussed.
- guided writing - small group sessions based on specific needs of a specific group of children. The session may address misconceptions, bridge gaps or extend learning and can take place at any point during the unit.

In addition, cross-curricular links are suggested, including links to challenges from the Learning Challenge Curriculum.

Possible Written Outcomes or Incidental Writing Opportunities

- Thought bubbles at key points in the story
- What makes a hero – explain
- Glossary of vocabulary
- Write the next chapter in Arthur's story
- Speech bubbles into dialogue from role play
- Description of monster to be overcome
- Use techniques identified to experiment with and craft a suspense paragraph
- Historical information text on the Vikings
- Fact files on Norse gods and monsters

YEAR 3 AND 4

Hook

- Leave a range of objects from the book in the classroom – golden rope, feather, a piece of parchment, cat's footprint
- Viking experience

Responding to the Text

Book talk: What do you think is going to happen in this book? Who do you think Arthur is? What do you think the golden rope will be for? Can you find any clues?
Book talk: Look at the blub: What do you think the Brownstone vault is?
Book talk: Use maps. Where is the story going to be set? What do the pictures around the outside of the maps tell you about the story? What symbol do you notice where Arthur's town is? What do you think the symbol represents and why might is be important? Why do you think there is a map of this in the front of the book?
Book talk: Do you think Arthur is going to be an unlikely hero? How do you think Arthur might be different?
Book talk: How would you describe Arthur's personality? What evidence is there?
Writer talk: Do you think this more a picture book or more like a comic? Explain your ideas.
Book talk: Why do you think the author Joe Todd-Stanton chose Arthur to be the main character?
Book talk: Do you think the story would have been different if somebody instead of Arthur had gone to find Thor?
Book talk: Has the writer any messages for the reader?

2. Capturing Ideas

- Gather information about the Vikings from the text
- Role on the wall for Arthur
- Gather ideas about the qualities of a hero – link to Arthur
- Freeze frame identified events and thought track – write thought bubbles
- Explore the plot of a quest story
- Collect examples of the techniques used to build suspense and keep the reader hooked
- Explore sentence types used in book, categorise and consider why they have been used
- Develop ideas for next chapter – what will he have to overcome, what magical object could he take (use illustration of vault to support) and how he will succeed
- Develop language to describe monster to be defeated
- Role play people discussing the problem and what might happen
- Use map or grid to plan new chapter
- Annotate plan with language developed
- Research Vikings and make notes

Sentence Games (use throughout unit)

- Sentence model from text to experiment with complex and multi-clause sentences
- Sentence starter game – ing and ed starters
- Adverbials sorting game
- Spotting apostrophes
- Use of illustration to name objects in vault and use possessive apostrophe to show ownership – Mr. Brownstone's, the Brownstones'

Guided Reading Possibilities

- Arthur and the Golden Rope
- Norse myths and legends
- Information books on the Vikings

3. Contextualised Grammar Teaching

- Adverbials collected from text and others listed and categorised
- Positioning and impact of adverbials in sentences or to introduce paragraphs
- Use of direct speech
- Consistency of tense

4. Modelled Writing
Shared Writing
Guided Writing
Independent Writing

MAKING LINKS ACROSS THE CURRICULUM

Geography/Science/History
- Use maps and atlases
- Plan a journey
- Understand the difference between a village and a city
- Vikings

Art/DT
- Look at comics and graphic novels and explore techniques used
- Design a page for the new chapter in Arthur's story

ICT

Music/PE

Useful links
https://www.bbc.co.uk/education/topics/ztyr9j6
https://www.jorvikvikingcentre.co.uk/education/national-curriculum/

Maths

Year 3 or 4 History:
Were the Vikings always victorious and vicious?

The Learning Challenge CURRICULUM

Author: Joe Todd Stanton
Publisher: Flying Eye Books
ISBN: 978-1-911171-03-4

Planning for Quality Texts: Gregory Cool

These documents are intended to support the planning of effective literacy units based on high quality books. They are not intended to be lesson plans, but offer a menu of possible ideas for teachers to use as Starting points to plan for purposeful learning and give pupils reasons for writing as well as the skills they need to write with impact on their reader. They follow a learning sequence:

- a hook to fully engage and interest the children
- responding to reading activities to allow immersion in and exploration of the text, including picture exploration, book and writer talk
- capturing ideas activities which include drama and talk to support understanding of the text and to develop vocabulary, language and ideas for writing
- possibilities for the contextualised teaching of grammar
- sentence games to develop creativity, vocabulary, language and grammar
- links to guided reading
- a range of writing tasks which may be final unit outcomes or incidental opportunities during the unit

Specific mention is made of the writing sequence:

- modelled writing - teacher models the writing process aloud and the decisions writers make about sentences, paragraphs etc. to create impact on the reader. This can also include the modelling of planning and spelling strategies.
- shared writing - collaborative composition with discussion and suggestions about what to write and how to write it to create the intended effect. At this point children may write a sentence/s, often in pairs, on whiteboards which are then discussed.
- guided writing - small group sessions based on specific needs of a specific group of children. The session may address misconceptions, bridge gaps or extend learning and can take place at any point during the unit.

In addition, cross-curricular links are suggested, including links to challenges from the Learning Challenge Curriculum.

YEAR 3 AND 4

Possible Written Outcomes or Incidental Writing Opportunities

- Predictions
- Information text on Tobago
- Tourist poster or leaflet advertising Tobago
- Comparison of house on Tobago and homes here
- Character descriptions of Gregory and Lennox
- Comparative text showing the differences and similarities between the two boys
- Description of view from hillside at the end of the book
- Writing in role – diary entries at key points in the story: arriving in Tobago and meeting grandparents, meeting Lennox, at the beach, the end of the book
- Letter from Gregory to his parents recounting his experience
- Glossary of vocabulary

Hook

- Illustration from text to discuss
- Objects – shell, sand, coconut etc.

Responding to the Text

Book talk: Use illustration on p1 with no text. Discuss what could be happening and where they might be. Repeat activity with front cover. Note differences. Predict what might have happened between the 2 illustrations.
Book talk: Use front page with illustration of plane. What other clues are there now? Where is this set?
Book talk: How does Gregory feel on his first evening on Tobago? How do you know? Use evidence from the text.
Book talk: Why do you think Gregory keeps using the word "cool"? What does this tell the reader about him?
Book talk: What do you think "the last thing he felt was cool" means?
Book talk: What makes Gregory begin to feel differently about life in Tobago?
Book talk: What evidence is there in the text that Gregory has changed his mind?
Book talk: Has the writer any messages for the reader?
Book talk: Have you ever been somewhere that you did not like, but changed your mind? Can you explain?
Writer talk: Find some words and language that show where this is set. Would the story be the same in another setting?

2. Capturing Ideas

- Find Tobago on a map
- Use range of sources to find out about Tobago
- Make notes
- Role play key scenes
- Freeze frame key scenes and thought track
- Annotate illustrations with thought and feelings bubbles
- Use Venn diagram or other graphic organiser to gather information from text about similarities between Lennox and Gregory and their lives
- Annotate with comparative language
- Annotate illustration of evening hillside with nouns, adjectives, verbs, prepositional phrases, adverbials

Sentence Games (use throughout unit)

- Sentence starter game – ing and ed starters
- Adverbials sorting game
- Spotting apostrophes
- Conjunctions game

Guided Reading Possibilities

- Gregory Cool
- A Caribbean Dozen – John Agard and Grace Nicholls
- Information on Tobago and the Caribbean

3. Contextualised Grammar Teaching

- Fronted adverbials to structure diary entries
- Show and not tell for Gregory
- Use of conjunctions to join similar ideas and give reasons
- Use of conjunctive adverbs to show differences
- Persuasive techniques

4. Modelled Writing
Shared Writing
Guided Writing
Independent Writing

MAKING LINKS ACROSS THE CURRICULUM

Geography/Science/History

- Use correct geographical words to describe a place and the things that happen there and identify the features of a locality using a map
- Plan a journey
- Understand the difference between a village and a City
- Use maps, atlases, globes and digital/ computer mapping to locate countries and describe features studied

Art/DT

ICT

- Research

Music/PE

- Find out about reggae music and Bob Marley

http://www.facts-about.org.uk/famous-people-facts-starting-with-b/bob-marley.htm

Useful links

http://www.infoplease.com/ipa/A0108046.html
http://www.mytobago.info/
http://travel.nationalgeographic.com/travel/countries/trinidad-tobago-facts/

Maths

Year 4 Geography: Where would you choose to build a city?

The Learning Challenge CURRICULUM

Author: Caroline Binch
Publisher: Frances Lincoln Ltd
ISBN: 978-0-7112-0880-2

Planning for Quality Texts: The Ice Palace

These documents are intended to support the planning of effective literacy units based on high quality books. They are not intended to be lesson plans, but offer a menu of possible ideas for teachers to use as Starting points to plan for purposeful learning and give pupils reasons for writing as well as the skills they need to write with impact on their reader. They follow a learning sequence:

- a hook to fully engage and interest the children
- responding to reading activities to allow immersion in and exploration of the text, including picture exploration, book and writer talk
- capturing ideas activities which include drama and talk to support understanding of the text and to develop vocabulary, language and ideas for writing
- possibilities for the contextualised teaching of grammar
- sentence games to develop creativity, vocabulary, language and grammar
- links to guided reading
- a range of writing tasks which may be final unit outcomes or incidental opportunities during the unit

Specific mention is made of the writing sequence:

- modelled writing - teacher models the writing process aloud and the decisions writers make about sentences, paragraphs etc. to create impact on the reader. This can also include the modelling of planning and spelling strategies.
- shared writing - collaborative composition with discussion and suggestions about what to write and how to write it to create the intended effect. At this point children may write a sentence/s, often in pairs, on whiteboards which are then discussed.
- guided writing - small group sessions based on specific needs of a specific group of children. The session may address misconceptions, bridge gaps or extend learning and can take place at any point during the unit.

In addition, cross-curricular links are suggested, including links to challenges from the Learning Challenge Curriculum.

Possible Written Outcomes or Incidental Writing Opportunities

- Note to parents explaining why Ivan has decided to go and find his brother
- Thought bubbles
- Feelings bubbles
- Note from old woman to Ivan
- Write in role as Ivan as he enters Starjik's palace and meets him
- Write in role as Ivan after he returns home
- Write in role as Starjik at the end of the book.
- List poem based on snow and ice, drawing on models from reading
- Glossary of vocabulary
- Non-chronological report (information leaflet)
- Instructions – How to survive in the snow
- Comparison with other stories

YEAR 3 AND 4

Hook

- Use first line – "If you turned your head into the east wind and you could see for ever you would see Ivan's land'
- Use images of snowy landscapes

Responding to the Text

Book talk: What is the effect of the first line of the book?
Writer talk: How does the writer show how the people feel?
Book talk: Why does Ivan gaze into the north for so long?
Book talk: What are your first impressions of Ivan? find evidence to support your ideas.
Book talk: Ivan has to overcome many dangers. Do you think Starjik is responsible? Give your reasons.
Book talk: Why do you think Ivan is so easily tricked by the dancing children?
Book talk: How does Ivan react to the old woman? Why do you think she has protected him?
Book talk: What is Ivan's reaction to seeing the children in Starjik's palace?
Book talk: What was the effect of the ice pips on Starjik? How does he change? What evidence is there that he will remain a good person?
Writer talk: How does the writer's use of descriptive language to create the setting help to create atmosphere?
Book talk: Does the story remind you of any others you have read? what are the links?

2. Capturing Ideas

- Collect words and language that writer uses to create the setting and emphasise the cold, snow and ice
- Role on the wall for Ivan
- Role on the wall for Starjik
- Add to role on wall as book is explored
- Create grid and note all the problems and dangers Ivan faces and the things that help him as book is read
- Gather feelings vocabulary
- Develop questions and interview old woman
- Listen to description of Starjik and his palace. Visualise and draw. Annotate with language from the text
- Hot seat Starjik
- Develop nouns, adjectives, verbs, similes, prepositional phrases for list poem
- Research animals that live in frozen environments and make notes
- Research other animals or plants and make notes

Sentence Games (use throughout unit)

- Prepositions game
- Sentence starter game – ing and ed starters
- Apostrophes – Ivan's, Starjik's, etc.
- Conjunctions game to join information or explain

Guided Reading Possibilities

- The Ice Palace
- The Snow Queen – Hans Christian Anderson
- Linked traditional stories – Hansel and Gretel, The Pied Piper etc.
- Information books on Polar regions

3. Contextualised Grammar Teaching

- Expanded noun phrases – before and after noun
- Similes for expanded noun phrases
- Precise word choices – clines for emotions vocabulary, zone of relevance
- First and third person
- Consistency of tense

4. Modelled Writing
Shared Writing
Guided Writing
Independent Writing

MAKING LINKS ACROSS THE CURRICULUM

Geography/Science/History

- Settlements, land use, economic activity including natural resources especially water supplies
- Identify and name a variety of living things (plants and animals) in the local and wider environment and group them

Art/DT

- Using range of materials to re-create snowy scenes as described in the book
- http://www.bbc.com/culture/story/20131224-the-10-greatest-winter-paintings

ICT

Music/PE

- Develop dance that children created in book – folk dancing

Useful links
http://www.wilderness-survival.net/chp15.php

PSHE

- Bravery and resilience

Year 4 Geography:
Where would you choose to build a city?
Year 4 Science:
Which plants and animals thrive in your locality?

The Learning Challenge
CURRICULUM

Author: Robert Swindells
Publisher: Puffin Books
ISBN: 978-0-14-034966-5

Planning with Quality Texts: Meerkat Mail

These documents are intended to support the planning of effective literacy units based on high quality picture books. They are not intended to be lesson plans, but offer a menu of possible ideas for teachers to use as starting points to plan for purposeful learning and give pupils reasons for writing as well as the skills they need to write with impact on their reader. They follow a learning sequence:

- a hook to fully engage and interest the children
- responding to reading activities to allow immersion in and exploration of the text, including picture exploration, book and writer talk
- capturing ideas activities which include drama and talk to support understanding of the text and to develop vocabulary, language and ideas for writing
- possibilities for the contextualised teaching of grammar
- sentence games to develop creativity, vocabulary, language and grammar
- links to guided reading
- a range of writing tasks which may be final unit outcomes or incidental opportunities during the unit

Specific mention is made of the writing sequence:

- modelled writing - teacher models the writing process aloud and the decisions writers make about sentences, paragraphs etc to create impact on the reader. This can also include the modelling of planning and spelling strategies.
- shared writing - collaborative composition with discussion and suggestions about what to write and how to write it to create the intended effect. At this point children may write a sentence/s, often in pairs, on whiteboards which are then discussed.
- guided writing - small group sessions based on specific needs of a specific group of children. The session may address misconceptions, bridge gaps or extend learning and can take place at any point during the unit.

In addition, cross-curricular links are suggested, including links to challenges from the Learning Challenge Curriculum.

Possible Written Outcomes or Incidental Writing Opportunities

- Postcard
- Email
- Thought/speech bubbles
- Fact file on meerkats
- Report on meerkats
- Letter to relative once he has returned home
- Newspaper report
- Passport/Identity card
- Label
- List
- Restaurant menu

YEAR 1,2,3 AND 4

Hook

- Postcard from Sunny to class
- Role play travelling to Africa and exploring
- Watch Meerkat Manor

1. Responding to the Text

- Watch clips from Meerkat Manor
- Picture exploration: Predicting possibilities, capture page in 2 adjectives, 2 verbs, 2 adverbs, turn the volume up - what might you hear?
- Story map/timeline of events or mapping journey
- Book talk: likes, dislikes, puzzles and reminders
- Writer talk: How does Emily Gravett show the reader how Sunny is feeling and his response to his adventures?
- Writer talk: How is the text organised?
- Writer talk: What types of sentences has Emily Gravett used? What is the effect?
- Writer talk: Look at word choices

2. Capturing Ideas

- Role play each visit
- Freeze frame role plays at different points
- Hot seat Sunny at different points in the story
- Back to back telephone call to family member
- Explore Sunny's feelings at different points in the story
- Make emotion graph to plot rise and fall of feelings
- Annotate graph with synonyms and use in explanatory sentence
- Generate when/where/how adverbials and annotate story map/timeline with possibilities
- Watch David Attenborough interviewing animal expert and identify question types and formal sentence structures for responses
- Role play interviewer/meerkat expert interview(could be filmed and evaluated)

Sentence Games (use throughout unit)

- Conjunctions game
- Warming up the word - generating synonyms for Sunny's feelings
- Improve a basic sentence using Emily Gravett's techniques
- Chain writing with "meerkats" as starting point. Develop according to grammar focus of unit and/or consolidation and practise of prior learning

Guided Reading Possibilities

- Read and explore other books by Emily Gravett and compare to Meerkat Mail
- Identify and discuss features of text type for final written outcome. Level of text can be pitched at each groups' level, ensuring both access and challenge.

3. Contextualised Grammar Teaching

- Explore use of comparative and superlative in text and how these are formed. Generate others from vocabulary generated by previous activities
- Develop expanded noun phrases
- Text is written in the present tense - explore changing to past tense. Investigation into past tense formation
- Use generated adverbials to experiment with creating different effects in sentences

4. Modelled Writing
Shared Writing
Guided Writing
Independent Writing

MAKING LINKS ACROSS THE CURRICULUM

Geography

- Use atlas/globe to find continent where meerkats live. Identify other continents.
- Use Google Earth to look at the places Sunny visits.
- Find places where meerkats could not live and look at location on globe/atlas
- How might you travel to any of these places?
- Which animals might you see?
- What food might you eat?

Science

- Investigate meerkat habitat
- Investigate other habitats and consider why they are suitable for particular creatures

Useful Links

- www.emilygravett.com
- www.animalplanet.co.uk
- http://www.literacyshed.com/the-photostory-shed.html
- www.earth.google.com

PSHE

- What do the meerkats in the story do?
- How is the meerkat family like a human family?
- Why are homes and families important to the meerkats and to us?
- Look at the meerkats' motto.
- What do you think Sunny thinks of the motto at the start of the story?
  How have his feelings changed by the end?
- Create a class motto

Year 1 Geography: Why can't a meerkat live at the North Pole?

The Learning Challenge
CURRICULUM

Author: Emily Gravett
Publisher: Macmillan Children's Books
ISBN: 978-1405090759

Planning for Quality Texts: The Tin Forest

These documents are intended to support the planning of effective literacy units based on high quality picture books. They are not intended to be lesson plans, but offer a menu of possible ideas for teachers to use as starting points to plan for purposeful learning and give pupils reasons for writing as well as the skills they need to write with impact on their reader. They follow a learning sequence:

- a hook to fully engage and interest the children
- responding to reading activities to allow immersion in and exploration of the text, including picture exploration, book and writer talk
- capturing ideas activities which include drama and talk to support understanding of the text and to develop vocabulary, language and ideas for writing
- possibilities for the contextualised teaching of grammar
- sentence games to develop creativity, vocabulary, language and grammar
- links to guided reading
- a range of writing tasks which may be final unit outcomes or incidental opportunities during the unit

Specific mention is made of the writing sequence:

- modelled writing - teacher models the writing process aloud and the decisions writers make about sentences, paragraphs etc to create impact on the reader. This can also include the modelling of planning and spelling strategies.
- shared writing - collaborative composition with discussion and suggestions about what to write and how to write it to create the intended effect. At this point children may write a sentence/s, often in pairs, on whiteboards which are then discussed.
- guided writing - small group sessions based on specific needs of a specific group of children. The session may address misconceptions, bridge gaps or extend learning and can take place at any point during the unit.

In addition, cross-curricular links are suggested, including links to challenges from the Learning Challenge Curriculum.

Possible Written Outcomes or Incidental Writing Opportunities

- Description of selected pictures from book
- Thought bubbles for old man at different points in the book
- Prequel to story - old man's life before he came to the rubbish dump
- Letter to an advice column
- Reply from advice column
- Poster for recycling
- Job advert for a helper for the old man
- Diary entry in role as old man
- Letter from old man about how he used the rubbish to make the forest
- My dream or hope for the future is... to put into class book of dreams
- Description of created environment based on different dreams
- List poem - In the forest of dreams...

YEAR 1,2,3 AND 4

Hook

- Boxes of recyclable material in classroom. Challenge children to make a plant or flower.
- Earth Song by Michael Jackson

1. Responding to the Text

- Visual literacy: use small picture on title page. Predict what the book might be about.
- Book talk: why does the old man make a forest from the rubbish?
- Book talk: what problems does the old man have?
- Book talk: what themes are in the book? (loneliness, loss, hope, perseverance)
- Book talk: what message is the writer trying to give the reader?
- Visual Literacy: how does the illustrator help the reader to understand how the forest became real?
- Book talk: why do you think the birds returned?
- Book talk: how do you feel at the end of the book? Can you explain your feelings?
- Writer talk: look at first sentence in book. What effect does she create? How does she do it?
- Writer talk: how does the writer use repeated language? What is the effect?

2. Capturing Ideas

- Think of questions to ask old man - life before he came to the dump, his hopes and dreams
- Hot seat old man
- Annotate pictures with nouns. Add detail - adjectives, verbs, adverbs etc
- Discuss own hopes and dreams
- The forest is the old man's dream. Collect ideas about how an environment would look with a different dream
- Visualise and sketch alternative environment
- Annotate as above
- Listen to or watch guided tour and identify language and "voice" used
- In role as guide, give guided tour to forest in book or new forest of dreams using the above
- Phone call to helpline for advice
- Role play a day in the life of the old man - list the jobs he does
- Interview candidates for job as helper to the old man
- Investigate school and local recycling procedures

Sentence Games (use throughout unit)

- Prepositions game
- Improve a sentence- focus on the grammatical elements that need consolidation or review
- Poetic sentences - In the forest of dreams...
- Chain writing

Guided Reading Possibilities

- A Child's Garden by Michael Foreman, Dinosaurs and All That Rubbish by Michael Foreman, The Flower by John Light. Look at similar themes and messages.
- Posters and leaflets on recycling
- Identify and discuss features of text type for final written outcome. Level of text can be pitched at each groups' level, ensuring both access and challenge.

3. Contextualised Grammar Teaching

- Expanded noun phrases
- Prepositions/prepositional phrases
- Adverbials of place
- Use of repeated language - words, phrases, clauses - and effects they create

4. Modelled Writing
Shared Writing
Guided Writing
Independent Writing

MAKING LINKS ACROSS THE CURRICULUM

Geography/Science
- Recycling
- Ecology
- Food chains

PSHE
- Dreams and aspirations

DT/ICT
- Use pictures from book or photographs of new created environment to make slide show
- Add voice over or commentary to make audio guide to the forest

Useful links
http://vimeo.com/36088583
http://www.literacyshed.com/the-photostory-shed.html

Art
- Make plants/flowers/animals or birds etc from recyclable materials to create a class "Tin Forest"
- Transform plastic pots into plant pots using collage techniques

Year 2 Science:
What is our school made of?
Year 3 Science:
How did that blossom become an apple?
Year 4 Science:
Which wild animals and plants thrive in your locality?

The Learning Challenge
CURRICULUM

Author: Helen Ward
Publisher: Templar
ISBN: 978-1-84011-743-1

Planning for Quality Texts: The Firebird

These documents are intended to support the planning of effective literacy units based on high quality books. They are not intended to be lesson plans, but offer a menu of possible ideas for teachers to use as starting points to plan for purposeful learning and give pupils reasons for writing as well as the skills they need to write with impact on their reader. They follow a learning sequence:

- a hook to fully engage and interest the children
- responding to reading activities to allow immersion in and exploration of the text, including picture exploration, book and writer talk
- capturing ideas activities which include drama and talk to support understanding of the text and to develop vocabulary, language and ideas for writing
- possibilities for the contextualised teaching of grammar
- sentence games to develop creativity, vocabulary, language and grammar
- links to guided reading
- a range of writing tasks which may be final unit outcomes or incidental opportunities during the unit

Specific mention is made of the writing sequence:

- modelled writing - teacher models the writing process aloud and the decisions writers make about sentences, paragraphs etc. to create impact on the reader. This can also include the modelling of planning and spelling strategies.
- shared writing - collaborative composition with discussion and suggestions about what to write and how to write it to create the intended effect. At this point children may write a sentence/s, often in pairs, on whiteboards which are then discussed.
- guided writing - small group sessions based on specific needs of a specific group of children. The session may address misconceptions, bridge gaps or extend learning and can take place at any point during the unit.

In addition, cross-curricular links are suggested, including links to challenges from the Learning Challenge Curriculum.

YEAR 4 AND 5

Possible Written Outcomes or Incidental Writing Opportunities

- Write in role as Ivan to his father at different points in the story
- List poem based on an illustration
- Letter to advice column from the wolf asking whether he should continue to help Ivan
- Reply from advice columnist giving advice to Grey Wolf
- Write an alternative ending supposing that Ivan had not tried to take the cage
- Write an additional quest for Ivan to complete
- Retell the story from Ivan's or from Grey Wolf's point of view
- Letter of apology from Ivan's brothers
- Argument - stating response to Is it ever right to steal?
- Non-chronological report on phoenixes

Hook

- Video clip of extract from The Firebird ballet
- Listen to Firebird music
-

1. Responding to the Text

- Book talk: Without revealing the front cover, read first three pages. What do we know about Ivan's character?
- Book talk: Read description of firebird several times. Visualise and draw. Compare with front cover.
- Book talk: Why do you think Grey Wolf returns to help Ivan? What do you think his role in the story might be?
- Book talk:
- Book talk: Do you know other stories like this one?
- Visual literacy: What is the impact of the illustrations on the story?
- Book talk: Is The Firebird the best title for the story? Can you think of another title?
- Book talk: Can you find clues to show when and where this is set?
- Writer talk: This is a traditional tale. Can you find clues in the language which show this?

2. Capturing Ideas

- Role on the wall for Prince Ivan - how other characters see him outside and his behaviour feeling and actions inside
- Conscience Alley - Which road should Ivan take? Use full sentences and reasons for choice
- Make a timeline or story map of the events
- Ivan had to undertake 3 quests. Invent another quest for him - what must he do? Where must he go? What will the role of Grey Wolf be?
- Add the quest to your timeline or story map
- What might have happened if Ivan had not tried to take the golden cage? Talk about how the story could have ended.
- Use an illustration, name 5 nouns and develop poetic sentences
- Put Ivan on trial for stealing the golden cage and the diamond bridle. Develop an argument for the prosecution and one for the defence.
- Debate - Is it ever right to steal?
- Research phoenixes
- Look at phoenixes in other stories - Harry Potter, The Phoenix and the Carpet
- Use a planning grid to organise information about phoenixes under sub-headings

Sentence Games (use throughout unit)

- Sentence starters game - focus on starters to be developed in contextualised teaching
- Persuasion game
- Change the atmosphere adjective game

Guided Reading Possibilities

- Read other versions of The Firebird. How are they similar? How are they different? Which version do you prefer? Why?
- Other books by Oliver Jeffers - Lost and Found, Stuck, How to Catch a Star
- Identify and discuss features of text type for final written outcome. Level of text can be pitched at each groups' level, ensuring both access and challenge.

3. Contextualised Grammar Teaching

- Vary sentence starters for impact - adverb, ing, ed
- Use of comma for adverb, ing, ed starters
- Power of three to expand sentence openers

4. Modelled Writing
Shared Writing
Guided Writing
Independent Writing

MAKING LINKS ACROSS THE CURRICULUM

Geography/Science/History
- Research Russia
- Research phoenix in Egyptian/Roman/Greek mythology

Music/Dance
- Listen and respond to Stravinsky's The Firebird. How does the music paint a picture of the firebird's movements
- Watch an extract from The Firebird ballet - http://www.youtube.com/watch?v=no2aPVEe0mA
- Create a firebird movement sequence

ICT

PSHE
- Ivan's father asks him to steal. Is it ever right to steal?

Useful links

http://www.youtube.com/watch?v=gY34G-utxs8
http://www.youtube.com/watch?v=IZm-9yx0uLo
http://www.youtube.com/watch?v=MHB3N88kl6E
http://www.youtube.com/watch?v=bSJ1suXiZ2I
http://www.youtube.com/watch?v=gi-KTJOEGhg

Art/DT
- Colour mixing to paint firebird
- Use of range of materials to create a textured collage of firebird

Year 5 Science:
Do all plants and animals start life as an egg?

The Learning Challenge CURRICULUM

Author: Saviour Pirotta
Publisher: Templar
ISBN: 978-1848771512

Planning for Quality Texts: Rose Blanche

These documents are intended to support the planning of effective literacy units based on high quality picture books. They are not intended to be lesson plans, but offer a menu of possible ideas for teachers to use as starting points to plan for purposeful learning and give pupils reasons for writing as well as the skills they need to write with impact on their reader. They follow a learning sequence:

- a hook to fully engage and interest the children
- responding to reading activities to allow immersion in and exploration of the text, including picture exploration, book and writer talk
- capturing ideas activities which include drama and talk to support understanding of the text and to develop vocabulary, language and ideas for writing
- possibilities for the contextualised teaching of grammar
- sentence games to develop creativity, vocabulary, language and grammar
- links to guided reading
- a range of writing tasks which may be final unit outcomes or incidental opportunities during the unit

Specific mention is made of the writing sequence:

- modelled writing - teacher models the writing process aloud and the decisions writers make about sentences, paragraphs etc to create impact on the reader. This can also include the modelling of planning and spelling strategies.
- shared writing - collaborative composition with discussion and suggestions about what to write and how to write it to create the intended effect. At this point children may write a sentence/s, often in pairs, on whiteboards which are then discussed.
- guided writing - small group sessions based on specific needs of a specific group of children. The session may address misconceptions, bridge gaps or extend learning and can take place at any point during the unit.

In addition, cross-curricular links are suggested, including links to challenges from the Learning Challenge Curriculum.

Possible Written Outcomes or Incidental Writing Opportunities

- Diary entry in role as Rose Blanche
- Diary entry in role as boy who tried to escape
- Letter of complaint to Mayor
- Note from Rose to her mother before her last visit to the camp
- Add dialogue to specific scenes
- Playscript of specific scenes
- Write more developed and detailed text for specific scenes
- Agony aunt column to advise Rose Blanche
- Extended description of specific scenes
- Discussion - What would I do to help someone in trouble?
- Information text on the White Rose movement in Germany
- Newspaper article about the disappearance of Rose Blanche
- Discussion - Did the townspeople behave well?

YEAR 4,5 AND 6

Hook

- Short clip from The Boy in The Striped Pyjamas of concentration camp

1. Responding to the Text

- Explore picture of Rose walking through the forest. What is happening? Start role on the wall.
- Explore the first 2 illustrations? Note thoughts.
- Find the clues that tell the reader where and when the story takes place
- How did Rose's thinking change through the story?
- What danger was Rose in? Why did she go on helping?
- What would you have done if you were Rose?
- Compare the illustration with Rose placing a flower on the barbed wire with the last picture showing the return of spring. Why did Innocenti decide to end the book with this picture? Why did he include the blue flower?
- Discuss the character of the mayor and how he may be perceived by the public.
- Why is there so little dialogue in the text? What do you notice about the punctuation of any dialogue? Why do you think it has been written in this way?
- How has the writer used adjectives and verbs? What is the impact?

2. Capturing Ideas

- Role play conversation between Rose and her mother – what may Rose ask and how will mother respond?
- Freeze Frame and thought track the incident with the mayor, the lorry and the boy.
- Freeze frame and thought track other scenes.
- Conscience Alley – What should Rose do? Help the children or ignore their needs?
- Interview Rose's mother and her friend to gather information.
- Role play conversations between characters.
- Research information about the holocaust/White Rose resistance movement.
- Build word banks

Sentence Games (use throughout unit)

- Play with different sentence starters - adjective, ing, ed, adverbial
- Improve a sentence - focus on the grammatical elements that need consolidation or review
- Experiment with verbs and adverbs for speech

Guided Reading Possibilities

- Read other diary extracts - Diary of Anne Frank, Archies' War
- More able readers (Y5 and 6)The Boy in the Striped Pyjamas
- Identify and discuss features of text type for final written outcome. Level of text can be pitched at each groups' level, ensuring both access and challenge.

3. Contextualised Grammar Teaching

- Review and consolidate direct speech
- Use of comma in direct speech
- Use of verbs and adverbs of speaker in direct speech
- Use of adverbials - how, when and where

4. Modelled Writing
Shared Writing
Guided Writing
Independent Writing

MAKING LINKS ACROSS THE CURRICULUM

History
- Wartime Germany
- The role of Hitler and the White Rose movement

PSHE
- Being responsible/caring for others
- Making choices and the impact of your choices
- Weighing up personal safety and the well-being of others

Art
- Paint contrasting images, using colours used by Innocenti and then the colours of spring
- Look at other Innocenti illustrations - The Last Resort

Useful links
- www.youtube.com/watch?v=cQVgniMcuoE
- http://www.bbc.co.uk/schools/primaryhistory/world_war2/children_at_war/

Year 5 History
How could Hitler have convinced a nation like Germany to follow him?

The Learning Challenge
CURRICULUM

Author: Ian McEwan
Publisher: Red Fox
ISBN: 978-0-099-43950-9

Planning for Quality Texts: Tuesday

These documents are intended to support the planning of effective literacy units based on high quality picture books. They are not intended to be lesson plans, but offer a menu of possible ideas for teachers to use as starting points to plan for purposeful learning and give pupils reasons for writing as well as the skills they need to write with impact on their reader. They follow a learning sequence:

- a hook to fully engage and interest the children
- responding to reading activities to allow immersion in and exploration of the text, including picture exploration, book and writer talk
- capturing ideas activities which include drama and talk to support understanding of the text and to develop vocabulary, language and ideas for writing
- possibilities for the contextualised teaching of grammar
- sentence games to develop creativity, vocabulary, language and grammar
- links to guided reading
- a range of writing tasks which may be final unit outcomes or incidental opportunities during the unit

Specific mention is made of the writing sequence:

- modelled writing - teacher models the writing process aloud and the decisions writers make about sentences, paragraphs etc to create impact on the reader. This can also include the modelling of planning and spelling strategies.
- shared writing - collaborative composition with discussion and suggestions about what to write and how to write it to create the intended effect. At this point children may write a sentence/s, often in pairs, on whiteboards which are then discussed.
- guided writing - small group sessions based on specific needs of a specific group of children. The session may address misconceptions, bridge gaps or extend learning and can take place at any point during the unit.

In addition, cross-curricular links are suggested, including links to challenges from the Learning Challenge Curriculum.

Possible Written Outcomes or Incidental Writing Opportunities

- Crime scene report
- Thought bubbles for frogs at different points
- Retell events from the point of view of one of the frogs
- Eye witness police report
- Newspaper report
- Summary of events
- Narrative action writing of dog chase event
- New event for frogs in the town
- Write text for book
- Instructions - How to fly a lily pad
- Write narrative with different creatures and different events
- Recount events to turtle
- Write story for a different audience - Reception class

YEAR 5

Hook

- Set up crime scene with lily pads
- Show video clip of book as CCTV with message from Chief Inspector seeking help in solving this crime

1. Responding to the Text

- Book talk: look at crime scene page. What evidence is there that something strange happened during the night?
- Book talk: what would you be thinking if you were one of the frogs as the lily pads rise into the air?
- Book talk: what would you think if you saw the frogs?
- Visual literacy: look at the picture of the frogs in the old lady's house. What are they doing? What does this tell you about their characters?
- Book talk: why do you think the lily pads stop floating?
- Book talk: how do the frogs get home? What might they say to each other?
- Book talk: what do you think might happen next Tuesday?
- Writer talk: the writer has only written times in the book. Why do you think this is?
- Writer talk: look at the writer's introduction to the book. What is the effect on the reader?

2. Capturing Ideas

- Set up Incident board with crime scene picture, witness pictures - man in dressing gown, turtle, dog and timeline with times from book
- Hot seat detective
- Look at pictures of different frogs - describe in no more than four words
- Each frog's feelings at different points in the story - build vocabulary (mesmerised, startled, exhilarated, astounded etc)
- Interview frog/s about experiences
- Word bank of flight/movement verbs and adverbs
- Interview witnesses - police and or reporter
- Telephone call from man in dressing gown to a friend explaining events
- Use pictures of dog chase - build toolkit of grammatical features of action writing
- Use map/mountain/boxing up to find structure of story
- Annotate with adverbials and topic sentences for each section
- Retell/present story orally
- Debate - Enchantment or not?

Sentence Games (use throughout unit)

- Capture the picture (use book illustrations) - in a verb and an adverb, an exclamation
- Turn the volume up for illustrations. Bilndfolded I heard? Focus on onomatopoeia.
- Sentence starters for basic sentence
- Improve a sentence- focus on the grammatical elements that need consolidation or review

Guided Reading Possibilities

- Other David Weisner books - Mr. Wuffles, Art and Max, Freefall. Develop inferential skills and giving opinions and justifying them.
- Use Tuesday to look at narrative plot structure. Compare with other narrative structures.
- Identify and discuss features of text type for final written outcome. Level of text can be pitched at each groups' level, ensuring both access and challenge.

3. Contextualised Grammar Teaching

- Time and place adverbials to make a cohesive narrative and link ideas between and across paragraphs
- Expanding adverbials - Late one clear evening, In the distance beyond the rolling fields…

4. Modelled Writing
Shared Writing
Guided Writing
Independent Writing

MAKING LINKS ACROSS THE CURRICULUM

Geography/Science
- Habitats
- Forensic techniques

DT/ICT
- Photostory for new event or story with different creatures
- Create illustration/s for story combining digital images with own illustrations

Useful links
http://www.youtube.com/watch?v=SINzoqgcHzw
http://www.literacyshed.com/the-picture-book-shed.html

PE
- Create a movement sequence based on the movement and flight vocabulary generated

Year 5 Science: Could you be the next CSI investigator?

The Learning Challenge CURRICULUM

Author: David Weisner
Publisher: Houghton Mifflin
ISBN- 978-0395870822

Planning for Quality Texts: The Incredible Book Eating Boy

These documents are intended to support the planning of effective literacy units based on high quality books. They are not intended to be lesson plans, but offer a menu of possible ideas for teachers to use as starting points to plan for purposeful learning and give pupils reasons for writing as well as the skills they need to write with impact on their reader. They follow a learning sequence:

- a hook to fully engage and interest the children
- responding to reading activities to allow immersion in and exploration of the text, including picture exploration, book and writer talk
- capturing ideas activities which include drama and talk to support understanding of the text and to develop vocabulary, language and ideas for writing
- possibilities for the contextualised teaching of grammar
- sentence games to develop creativity, vocabulary, language and grammar
- links to guided reading
- a range of writing tasks which may be final unit outcomes or incidental opportunities during the unit

Specific mention is made of the writing sequence:

- modelled writing - teacher models the writing process aloud and the decisions writers make about sentences, paragraphs etc to create impact on the reader. This can also include the modelling of planning and spelling strategies.
- shared writing - collaborative composition with discussion and suggestions about what to write and how to write it to create the intended effect. At this point children may write a sentence/s, often in pairs, on whiteboards which are then discussed.
- guided writing - small group sessions based on specific needs of a specific group of children. The session may address misconceptions, bridge gaps or extend learning and can take place at any point during the unit.

In addition, cross-curricular links are suggested, including links to challenges from the Learning Challenge Curriculum.

Possible Written Outcomes or Incidental Writing Opportunities

- Retell the story with more developed and detailed text
- Diary entry/ email from one of Henry's parents about the problem
- Description of a meal of books
- Book recommendation/podcast
- Write a new version - The Incredible computer/Xbox/car etc. Eating Boy/Girl
- Poster to advertise a circus performance by the Book Eating Boy
- Explanation - how the digestive system works
- Recipe for a healthy meal
- Devise a crossword
- Medical report from doctor
- Letter to Henry telling him about the importance of eating a healthy diet

YEAR 5

Hook

- Library visit
- Science related visit
- Show adapted animation

1. Responding to the Text

- Visual literacy: Look at the front cover? Does it remind you of anything?
- Book talk: What can you find out about Henry's character? What do you think his life was like before he started eating books?
- Visual literacy: The writer has used many different kinds of paper as background. Why do you think he did this? What effect does it have?
- Visual literacy: How do the pictures help to add detail to the story?
- Book talk: What message do you think Oliver Jeffers is trying to give us in this book?
- Book talk: Who told Henry to stop eating books? Did they give him good reasons? Why do you think he stopped?
- Book talk: Henry starts by eating a word and then a sentence. Which word and sentence would you choose to eat?
- Book talk: How does Henry feel between stopping eating books and reading them?

2. Capturing Ideas

- Find as many different types of books as possible, list and find examples of each type.
- Discuss which types of books they prefer and explain why
- Discuss how different books might taste and build a word bank
- If they were a book eater, which book would they eat and why
- Talk about favourite book and why they would recommend it to a friend
- Interview Henry's parents about his book eating and how they feel
- Phone call to Henry to persuade him not eat books
- Talk about what might happen to Henry if his dream of being eaten by a book came true
- Plan a menu to encourage Henry to eat something different
- Henry knows more than his teacher. What would they teach the teacher? Use of modal language - If I… I would/might/could…

Sentence Games (use throughout unit)

- Sentence starters game - focus on starters to be developed in contextualised teaching
- Chain writing with a focus on adding effective detail to sentences
- Adjectives with talent game - choosing the best adjective for sentences to describe the taste of different books

Guided Reading Possibilities

- Explore different book genres. How do we recognise them? Structure, characters, setting. Close reading of openings to books for clues about genre
- Other books by Oliver Jeffers - Lost and Found, Stuck, How to Catch a Star
- Identify and discuss features of text type for final written outcome. Level of text can be pitched at each groups' level, ensuring both access and challenge.

3. Contextualised Grammar Teaching

- Vary sentence starters for impact - adverb, ing, ed
- Use of comma for adverb, ing, ed starters
- Paragraphing

4. Modelled Writing
Shared Writing
Guided Writing
Independent Writing

MAKING LINKS ACROSS THE CURRICULUM

Geography/Science/History	Maths	ICT
• Link to Science - life cycles	• Survey of favourite books • List books Henry might have eaten as a meal. Research how much they may have cost. Find the cost of a healthy meal. How would this compare? How much would a week of meals cost? What would the difference be?	• Design a front cover for a delicious and a disgusting book, choosing the most effective font • •
PSHE • Henry feels clever in the story when he has eaten lots of books. He doesn't have to work or try hard to know things. Discuss how important it is to always try.		**Useful links** http://www.youtube.com/watch?v=gY34G-utxs8
Art/DT • Design a front cover for a delicious and a disgusting book • Paint backgrounds for the naughty bus' adventures • Use different tyres to create prints and patterns	**Year 5 Science: Do all plants and animals start life as an egg?**	The Learning Challenge CURRICULUM
Author: Oliver Jeffers **Publisher:** Harper Collins **ISBN:** 978-0-00-749093-6		

Planning for Quality Texts: Brother Eagle, Sister Sky

These documents are intended to support the planning of effective literacy units based on high quality books. They are not intended to be lesson plans, but offer a menu of possible ideas for teachers to use as starting points to plan for purposeful learning and give pupils reasons for writing as well as the skills they need to write with impact on their reader. They follow a learning sequence:

- a hook to fully engage and interest the children
- responding to reading activities to allow immersion in and exploration of the text, including picture exploration, book and writer talk
- capturing ideas activities which include drama and talk to support understanding of the text and to develop vocabulary, language and ideas for writing
- possibilities for the contextualised teaching of grammar
- sentence games to develop creativity, vocabulary, language and grammar
- links to guided reading
- a range of writing tasks which may be final unit outcomes or incidental opportunities during the unit

Specific mention is made of the writing sequence:

- modelled writing - teacher models the writing process aloud and the decisions writers make about sentences, paragraphs etc. to create impact on the reader. This can also include the modelling of planning and spelling strategies.
- shared writing - collaborative composition with discussion and suggestions about what to write and how to write it to create the intended effect. At this point children may write a sentence/s, often in pairs, on whiteboards which are then discussed.
- guided writing - small group sessions based on specific needs of a specific group of children. The session may address misconceptions, bridge gaps or extend learning and can take place at any point during the unit.

In addition, cross-curricular links are suggested, including links to challenges from the Learning Challenge Curriculum.

Possible Written Outcomes or Incidental Writing Opportunities
- Report on an aspect of American Indian life
- Balanced argument - We are destroying our planet
- Biography of a known figure committed to conservation and preservation of the earth
- Letter to Chief Seattle giving opinion on his speech
- Report on environmental issue researched
- Transform environmental issue report into a speech in the style of Chief Seattle

YEAR 5

Hook
- Show montage of before and after pictures of places where the natural environment has been changed by our lack of care
- Show Michael Jackson Earth Song video - http://www.youtube.com/watch?v=VqeADZgjtpY

1. Responding to the Text
- Book talk: Chief Seattle asks how can you buy the sky? What do you think he means? Why might he have said this?
- Book talk: Do you think Chief Seattle had an idea of what might happen to the environment?
- Book talk: What was he trying to say when he said that we did not weave the web of life? We are merely one thread in it?
- Book talk: What do you think was the writer's purpose in producing this book?
- Book talk: What sort of person do you think Chief Seattle was?
- Book talk: Can you find evidence from the book to show how Chief Seattle and his people viewed the earth?
- Writer talk: What does Chief Seattle compare the earth to? Can you find examples of this in the text? Why does he do this?
- Writer talk: How does Chief Seattle appeal to his audience? What techniques does he use?
- Visual literacy: How do the paintings reinforce the message/theme of the book?

2. Capturing Ideas
- Use a venn diagram to compare the role of a mother and the role of the earth
- Interview Chief Seattle
- Choose a section of Chief Seattle's speech and perform it
- Can you find any people like Chief Seattle with concerns about the environment in the present or recent past?
- Give a short oral presentation about the person researched using formal standard English
- Research places where American Indians live/lived and their way of life. Record and organise your information
- Discuss current environmental issues
- Choose one, research it and note and organise the information into a planning format
- Annotate the plan with detail to appeal to the reader/listener
- Use Chief Seattle's techniques to explain your issue to a partner or a group
- Debate - We are destroying our planet

Sentence Games (use throughout unit)
- Persuasion game
- Messing with modals game
- Sorting the subjunctive game
- Adjectives with talent game - changing the atmosphere

Guided Reading Possibilities
- Other quotes from Chief Seattle inference deduction, language choices
- Hiawatha narrative poem by Longfellow
- Identify and discuss features of text type for final written outcome. Level of text can be pitched at each groups' level, ensuring both access and challenge.

3. Contextualised Grammar Teaching
- Modality to establish a strong point of view and engage the reader
- Use of subjunctive to show possibility and wishes
- Paragraphing

4. Modelled Writing
Shared Writing
Guided Writing
Independent Writing

MAKING LINKS ACROSS THE CURRICULUM

Geography/Science/History
- Compare the local environment now with the environment over 100 years ago
- Investigate soil erosion/acid rain/deforestation etc.

Maths

ICT
- Film speeches and evaluate impact and quality of language

PSHE
- Environmental issues

Useful links
http://www.youtube.com/watch?v=milJHghldll
http://www.youtube.com/watch?v=MuJzMu6u-pg

Art/DT
- Look at American Indian art

Year 5/6 Geography:
What is so special about the USA?

The Learning Challenge
CURRICULUM

Author: Susan Jeffers
Publisher: Puffin Books
ISBN: 978-0140-545142

Planning for Quality Texts: Think of an Eel

These documents are intended to support the planning of effective literacy units based on high quality books. They are not intended to be lesson plans, but offer a menu of possible ideas for teachers to use as starting points to plan for purposeful learning and give pupils reasons for writing as well as the skills they need to write with impact on their reader. They follow a learning sequence:

- a hook to fully engage and interest the children
- responding to reading activities to allow immersion in and exploration of the text, including picture exploration, book and writer talk
- capturing ideas activities which include drama and talk to support understanding of the text and to develop vocabulary, language and ideas for writing
- possibilities for the contextualised teaching of grammar
- sentence games to develop creativity, vocabulary, language and grammar
- links to guided reading
- a range of writing tasks which may be final unit outcomes or incidental opportunities during the unit

Specific mention is made of the writing sequence:

- modelled writing - teacher models the writing process aloud and the decisions writers make about sentences, paragraphs etc to create impact on the reader. This can also include the modelling of planning and spelling strategies.
- shared writing - collaborative composition with discussion and suggestions about what to write and how to write it to create the intended effect. At this point children may write a sentence/s, often in pairs, on whiteboards which are then discussed.
- guided writing - small group sessions based on specific needs of a specific group of children. The session may address misconceptions, bridge gaps or extend learning and can take place at any point during the unit.

In addition, cross-curricular links are suggested, including links to challenges from the Learning Challenge Curriculum.

Possible Written Outcomes or Incidental Writing Opportunities

- Explanation - the life cycle of chosen creature
- Labelled life cycle diagram
- Experimental paragraphs working on use of figurative language, different sentence types and evaluate effectiveness
- Think of an … Life cycle written in the same style as the writer
- Life cycle written for a younger audience. For example - Reception class
- List poem based on eel or researched creature or plant
- Praise poem based on eel or researched creature or plant

YEAR 5

Hook

- Watch video - http://www.youtube.com/watch?v=UHEy9RXaHds
- Visit to zoo, river, wild life park

1. Responding to the Text

- Book talk: Initial impressions from front cover and introduction by writer? What kind of book is this?
- Book talk: Having read book, do you think it gives the information well? Do you like the style and language use?
- Visual literacy: How do the illustrations contribute to the book? Do they add information? Are they what you expect to see in a non-fiction text?
- Book talk: What would you expect to see in a non-fiction text on this subject? Does this book do the same job?
- Writer talk: Can you find the language and grammatical features the writer has used? Can you list them and find some examples?
- Writer talk: What is the effect of the use of these features on us as readers?
- Writer talk: What sentence types does the writer use? Can you spot examples?
- Book talk: Would you recommend this book to someone who wanted information about eels? Why/not? What else could you learn from the book?

2. Capturing Ideas

- Find all the facts about eels from the book
- Map the life cycle on to a graphic organiser
- Annotate with specific, technical vocabulary
- Annotate each phase with linking devices - adverbials (how, when and where), connecting adverbs
- Retell the life cycle to a partner/group in scientific language in complete sentences
- Research another creature or plant and note key information
- Add information to life cycle graphic organiser, checking for scientific, precise vocabulary. Add linking devices to each phase
- Discuss and build a word bank of descriptive language for chosen creature or plant, drawing on the features used by the writer - simile, metaphor, strong verbs, alliteration and annotate plan
- Using different sentence types and starters, annotate plan with a topic sentence for each phase's paragraph
- Rehearse orally in full sentences

Sentence Games (use throughout unit)

- Simile game
- Metaphor game
- Alliteration game
- Improve a sentence

Guided Reading Possibilities

- Focus on poetry and poetic language both from book and from poems about creatures. For example - Bluebottle by Judith Nicholls, Frog by Norman Maccaig etc.
- Non-fiction books with life cycle information. Focus on organisation and structure.
- Identify and discuss features of text type for final written outcome. Level of text can be pitched at each groups' level, ensuring both access and challenge.

3. Contextualised Grammar Teaching

- Figurative language - simile, metaphor
- Use of different sentence types for impact
- Developing a topic sentence to open paragraphs

4. Modelled Writing
Shared Writing
Guided Writing
Independent Writing

MAKING LINKS ACROSS THE CURRICULUM

Geography/Science/History
- Link to Science - life cycles
- Habitats and journeys undertaken by living things

Maths

ICT
- Make a PowerPoint or Photo Story with a voice over to present the life cycle of a creature

PSHE
- Discuss life cycles and the link to the human life cycle and death. Could read The Gift by Carol Ann Duffy

Useful links
http://www.youtube.com/watch?v=UHEy9RXaHds
http://www.youtube.com/watch?v=AMs3waaW75g
http://watchdocumentary.org/watch/natures-great-events-episode-02-the-great-salmon-run-video_fa7a91b66.html

Art/DT
- Draw or paint pictures to enhance or reinforce the life cycle information
- Combine with photographs

Year 5 Science: Do all plants and animals start life as an egg?

The Learning Challenge CURRICULUM

Author: Karen Wallace
Publisher: Walker Books
ISBN: 978-1-4063-1202-7

Planning for Quality Texts: Cloud Tea Monkeys

These documents are intended to support the planning of effective literacy units based on high quality picture books. They are not intended to be lesson plans, but offer a menu of possible ideas for teachers to use as starting points to plan for purposeful learning and give pupils reasons for writing as well as the skills they need to write with impact on their reader. They follow a learning sequence:

- a hook to fully engage and interest the children
- responding to reading activities to allow immersion in and exploration of the text, including picture exploration, book and writer talk
- capturing ideas activities which include drama and talk to support understanding of the text and to develop vocabulary, language and ideas for writing
- possibilities for the contextualised teaching of grammar
- sentence games to develop creativity, vocabulary, language and grammar
- links to guided reading
- a range of writing tasks which may be final unit outcomes or incidental opportunities during the unit

Specific mention is made of the writing sequence:

- modelled writing - teacher models the writing process aloud and the decisions writers make about sentences, paragraphs etc to create impact on the reader. This can also include the modelling of planning and spelling strategies.
- shared writing - collaborative composition with discussion and suggestions about what to write and how to write it to create the intended effect. At this point children may write a sentence/s, often in pairs, on whiteboards which are then discussed.
- guided writing - small group sessions based on specific needs of a specific group of children. The session may address misconceptions, bridge gaps or extend learning and can take place at any point during the unit.

In addition, cross-curricular links are suggested, including links to challenges from the Learning Challenge Curriculum.

Possible Written Outcomes or Incidental Writing Opportunities

- TV/Radio advert for Cloud Tea
- Report on tea growing
- Retell of legend of monkeys who pick tea
- Use illustration to write a descriptive paragraph/s using sentence structures of book opening as a model
- Newspaper report about the monkeys which pick cloud tea
- Parallel recounts of scene with Royal Tea-Taster from different points of view - overseer, Sonam, monkeys, Tashi
- Royal proclamation about the discovery of cloud tea
- Note from Tashi to the monkeys, thanking them for their help
- Letter to overseer from tea-pickers requesting better conditions and treatment
- Rewrite story with different crop and creature coming to Tashi's rescue

YEAR 5 AND 6

Hook

- Tea making and tasting
- Watch video of tea-picking/growing (see useful links)

1. Responding to the Text

- Visual Literacy: how do the illustrations help us to understand the time of day?
- Visual literacy: there are coloured illustrations and some small pen and ink drawings. Why do you think the illustrator has done this?
- Book talk: find clues that tell the reader that this story is set in another place and time
- Book talk: Have you any questions about the story? Does it remind you of anything?
- Book talk: what does Tashi discover as a result of her kindness to the monkeys?
- Book talk: what might be the themes in this book?
- Writer talk: look at the way in which the writers use descriptive language to create pictures in the reader's head. What grammatical features have they used?
- Writer talk: look at how the writers have used action, description and dialogue. How does this tell the reader about the characters and their feelings and reactions
- Writer talk: look at the types of sentences the writers have used. What is the effect?

2. Capturing Ideas

- Identify the key events in the story
- Research the legend of tea-picking monkeys and record the main points
- Retell the legend orally
- Research the growing of tea and text mark relevant information
- Collate and organise information under sub-headings
- Role play scene with Royal Tea-Taster. Freeze frame and thought track each of the characters
- Organise a tea tasting
- Role play reporter live on the scene following the departure of the Royal Tea-Taster
- Debate - Sack the overseer?
- What if activity - what if they had been picking another crop? What if another creature had helped Tashi?
- Use planning format - map, mountain boxing up to plan in changes

Sentence Games (use throughout unit)

- Simile game
- Metaphor game
- Complex sentence game
- Improve a sentence- focus on the grammatical elements that need consolidation or review

Guided Reading Possibilities

- Cloud Tea Monkeys. Look at quality of language, discuss effects. Collect words etc.
- Information books on India, tea growing
- Identify and discuss features of text type for final written outcome. Level of text can be pitched at each groups' level, ensuring both access and challenge.

3. Contextualised Grammar Teaching

- Simile and metaphor to create effective description which creates a picture for the reader
- Semi-colon in a sentence to describe and add detail
- Developing characterisation through action, description and dialogue - showing not telling

4. Modelled Writing
Shared Writing
Guided Writing
Independent Writing

MAKING LINKS ACROSS THE CURRICULUM

Geography/Science
- Investigate India and the Himalayas
- Fair trade tea

History
- History of tea - cultivation, drinking etc

DT/ICT
- Create slideshow with voice-over on process of tea production

PSHE
- Child labour - look at children in other countries who work and do not attend school

Useful links
http://vimeo.com/66260870
http://www.britishpathe.com/video/the-story-of-india-tea
http://www.youtube.com/watch?v=ZJFaYKEDle4

Art
- Pen and ink line drawings in the style of the Illustrator

The Learning Challenge
CURRICULUM

Author: Mal Peet and Elspeth Graham
Publisher: Walker Books
ISBN: 978-1-4063-0092-5

Planning for Quality Texts: The Princess' Blankets

These documents are intended to support the planning of effective literacy units based on high quality picture books. They are not intended to be lesson plans, but offer a menu of possible ideas for teachers to use as starting points to plan for purposeful learning and give pupils reasons for writing as well as the skills they need to write with impact on their reader. They follow a learning sequence:

- a hook to fully engage and interest the children
- responding to reading activities to allow immersion in and exploration of the text, including picture exploration, book and writer talk
- capturing ideas activities which include drama and talk to support understanding of the text and to develop vocabulary, language and ideas for writing
- possibilities for the contextualised teaching of grammar
- sentence games to develop creativity, vocabulary, language and grammar
- links to guided reading
- a range of writing tasks which may be final unit outcomes or incidental opportunities during the unit

Specific mention is made of the writing sequence:

- modelled writing - teacher models the writing process aloud and the decisions writers make about sentences, paragraphs etc to create impact on the reader. This can also include the modelling of planning and spelling strategies.
- shared writing - collaborative composition with discussion and suggestions about what to write and how to write it to create the intended effect. At this point children may write a sentence/s, often in pairs, on whiteboards which are then discussed.
- guided writing - small group sessions based on specific needs of a specific group of children. The session may address misconceptions, bridge gaps or extend learning and can take place at any point during the unit.

In addition, cross-curricular links are suggested, including links to challenges from the Learning Challenge Curriculum.

YEAR 5 AND 6

Possible Written Outcomes or Incidental Writing Opportunities

- Create and describe another natural blanket in the writer's style
- Re-write the ending with a different successful stranger
- Create your own traditional story based upon the Princess's Blankets, keeping the pattern of 4.
- Write the ending from more than one different point of view - princess, king, stranger, musician.
- Newspaper report about the catastrophic events that are happening in in the princess' kingdom
- Newspaper report with bias - from unsuccessful stranger's point of view or princess' point of view
- Petition to king to stop depleting the earth of all its resources
- Letter to an agony aunt in role as the princess
- Reply to letter in role as agony aunt
- Dialogue added to scenes
- Play script of key scene/s

Hook

- Display board prepared with string to make weaving loom and strips of different materials for pupils to weave into a blanket
- Watch clip from Frozen where Anna is frozen and Elsa understands that love will melt the ice she has created

1. Responding to the Text

- Book talk: Make predictions from cover.
- Book talk: What type of text could it be? What do we know already about this text type?
- Create Venn diagram to compare/contrast with known traditional tales
- Book talk: find key narrative language and list
- Book talk: which traditional stories do you know that have suitors seeking to marry a princess?
- Hot seat the princess, the king and queen, the stranger and the musician and make role on the wall. Note their thoughts, reactions and opinions of each other.
- Visualise and draw blanket from description read aloud
- Writer talk: Look at the vocabulary and language used to describe the blankets. Explore under headings -felt, woven in, smelled of, in its borders, embroidered with, patterned with. What is the impact?
- Writer talk: How has the writer achieved this impact? Which grammatical features has she used?
- Writer talk: How has the writer shown the reader how the princess feels?

2. Capturing Ideas

- Create grid and note problems created by the blankets. Which resources were used and what were the consequences?
- Compare descriptions of different blankets, noting word choice and grammatical features used.
- Identify sentence structures used and make a talk planner/speaking frame
- Develop ideas for a new blanket. What would the problems be? Which resources used and what would the consequences be? What would the princess' reaction be?
- Develop descriptive language for new blanket under heading already used. Identify nouns, verbs. Develop to expanded noun phrases, adverbials, simile, metaphor.
- Use talk planner to experiment with creating an oral description. Rehearse evaluate and adapt description to create the most impact.
- Interview main characters to get their perspective on events
- Create new character to solve problem
- Role play scenes with new character

Sentence Games (use throughout unit)

- Simile game
- Metaphor game
- Add detail to a base sentence which shows rather than tells the reader about a character - *The princess lay in bed.*
- Playing with different sentence starters for a base sentence

Guided Reading Possibilities

- Read traditional tales and compare the key language, patterns, structure and features
- Read other books by Carol Ann Duffy and compare use of language, grammatical features and word choices
- Identify and discuss features of text type for final written outcome. Level of text can be pitched at each groups' level, ensuring both access and challenge.

3. Contextualised Grammar Teaching

- Expanded noun phrases with precise word choices
- Commas to clarify meaning, to add extra information in detailed sentences
- Complex sentences with more than one subordinate clause and embedding ing and ed non-finite subordinate clauses
- Choice and control of specific language features to create an effect

4. Modelled Writing

Shared Writing
Guided Writing
Independent Writing

MAKING LINKS ACROSS THE CURRICULUM

Geography/Science
- Environmental issues - pollution, global warming, de-forestation
- Food chains and interdependence

DT/ICT
- Video character interviews and make into a news item for 6 o'clock news

PSHE
- Environmental issues - debating

Art
- Create blankets from a range of materials
- Use stitching and embroidery on textiles to add to blanket design

The Learning Challenge
CURRICULUM

Author: Carol Ann Duffy
Publisher: Templar Books
ISBN: 978-0763645472

Planning for Quality Texts: Shackleton's Journey

These documents are intended to support the planning of effective literacy units based on high quality books. They are not intended to be lesson plans, but offer a menu of possible ideas for teachers to use as starting points to plan for purposeful learning and give pupils reasons for writing as well as the skills they need to write with impact on their reader. They follow a learning sequence:

- a hook to fully engage and interest the children
- responding to reading activities to allow immersion in and exploration of the text, including picture exploration, book and writer talk
- capturing ideas activities which include drama and talk to support understanding of the text and to develop vocabulary, language and ideas for writing
- possibilities for the contextualised teaching of grammar
- sentence games to develop creativity, vocabulary, language and grammar
- links to guided reading
- a range of writing tasks which may be final unit outcomes or incidental opportunities during the unit

Specific mention is made of the writing sequence:

- modelled writing - teacher models the writing process aloud and the decisions writers make about sentences, paragraphs etc. to create impact on the reader. This can also include the modelling of planning and spelling strategies.
- shared writing - collaborative composition with discussion and suggestions about what to write and how to write it to create the intended effect. At this point children may write a sentence/s, often in pairs, on whiteboards which are then discussed.
- guided writing - small group sessions based on specific needs of a specific group of children. The session may address misconceptions, bridge gaps or extend learning and can take place at any point during the unit.

In addition, cross-curricular links are suggested, including links to challenges from the Learning Challenge Curriculum.

Possible Written Outcomes or Incidental Writing Opportunities

- Job description of role including skills and personal qualities
- Letter of application for job
- Advert for ship
- Ship's log at key points in journey - in role or 3rd person narration
- Writing in role as one of dogs at different points in the journey
- Write descriptive text for illustrations. For example: p45 and 46 or p49 and 50
- Develop dialogue between characters
- Journalistic writing
- Descriptive paragraphs for obstacles met on journey
- Adventure story based on journey from Elephant Island to the whaling station
- Non-chronological report on chosen Antarctic creatures
- Poetry based on snow/ice

YEAR 5 AND 6

Hook

- Use Shackleton's original advert -

MEN WANTED
For hazardous journey, small wages, bitter cold, long months of complete darkness, constant danger, safe return doubtful, honour and recognition in case of success.

- Use photograph of stranded ship to discuss what, when, where, why

http://www.britannica.com/topic/Endurance-British-ship

Responding to the Text

- Book talk: Use front cover. What might the book be about?
- Book talk: Double page of crew. Discuss different roles on board.
- Book talk: Double page of dogs. Why might names have been chosen?
- Book talk: How important were all the crew members? Might some have had more important roles than others?
- Book talk: What influenced the choice of the route taken? Were there other options?
- Writer talk: What is the role of the illustrations?
- Writer talk: Gather words and language that William Grill uses to describe the snow and ice. Discuss their effectiveness and why Grill used them.
- Writer talk: What impression does the writer give when he uses the phrase "against all the odds" p61?
- Book talk: Discuss the quote on P.66. Do you believe that Shackleton was right?

2. Capturing Ideas

- Conscience alley - should you apply for job?
- Map of journey with timeline of events
- Fortune graph annotated with events and sailors' feelings
- Fortune graph annotated with events and dogs' feelings
- Hot seating of Shackleton
- Freeze frame and thought track identified scenes
- Role play interactions between characters as identified points in the story
- Thought bubbles and speech bubbles showing the difference between thoughts and words
- Research hazards and obstacles encountered on journey
- Research other possible hazards/obstacles
- Build word banks for obstacles
- Research Antarctic creatures

Sentence Games (use throughout unit)

- Subjunctive game - If you were to employ me..., The position requires that...
- Ranking of modal verbs
- Cline activity - cold adjectives
- Zone of relevance - movement verbs

Guided Reading Possibilities

- Shackleton's Journey
- Information books on Antarctica
- Archived material on Shackleton and the voyage
- Film resources – see links below
- Poem – Snow by Walter de la Mare

3. Contextualised Grammar Teaching

- Use of verbs to show and not tell emotions
- Building paragraphs with action, description and dialogue
- Topic sentences/adverbials to signal changes in time, place, event
- Modal verbs to develop a persuasive argument
- Adding modal adverbs to strengthen argument

4. Modelled Writing
Shared Writing
Guided Writing
Independent Writing

MAKING LINKS ACROSS THE CURRICULUM

Geography/Science/History
- Mapping journey
- Map skills, grid references
- Physical features of Antarctic and comparison with other zones
- Research Shackleton and other explorers Amundsen, Scott
- Compare Shackleton and Scott

Maths
- Calculate provisions required for crew
- Distances covered
- Calculating the shortest routes
- Link to Simon Beck's art based on mathematical designs

ICT
- Research archived material

Music/PE
-
-
-

Useful links
https://www.youtube.com/watch?v=sgh_77TtX5I
https://www.youtube.com/watch?v=JbRvegcbyxU&feature=youtu.be
http://williamgrill.co.uk/Shackleton-s-Journey-1
https://emmalkerr.wordpress.com/2013/01/26/shackleton-resources-history/
http://www.discoveringantarctica.org.uk/
The Endurance - DVD

Art/DT
- Explore Simon Beck's snow art
- Compare The Sea of Ice by Caspar David Friedrich with the illustrations in the text

Year 6 Geography:
I am a Year 6 pupil; Can you get me out of here?

The Learning Challenge CURRICULUM

Author: William Grill
Publisher: Flying Eye Books
ISBN: 978-1-909263-10-9

Planning for Quality Texts: The Lost Thing

These documents are intended to support the planning of effective literacy units based on high quality books. They are not intended to be lesson plans, but offer a menu of possible ideas for teachers to use as starting points to plan for purposeful learning and give pupils reasons for writing as well as the skills they need to write with impact on their reader. They follow a learning sequence:

- a hook to fully engage and interest the children
- responding to reading activities to allow immersion in and exploration of the text, including picture exploration, book and writer talk
- capturing ideas activities which include drama and talk to support understanding of the text and to develop vocabulary, language and ideas for writing
- possibilities for the contextualised teaching of grammar
- sentence games to develop creativity, vocabulary, language and grammar
- links to guided reading
- a range of writing tasks which may be final unit outcomes or incidental opportunities during the unit

Specific mention is made of the writing sequence:

- modelled writing - teacher models the writing process aloud and the decisions writers make about sentences, paragraphs etc. to create impact on the reader. This can also include the modelling of planning and spelling strategies.
- shared writing - collaborative composition with discussion and suggestions about what to write and how to write it to create the intended effect. At this point children may write a sentence/s, often in pairs, on whiteboards which are then discussed.
- guided writing - small group sessions based on specific needs of a specific group of children. The session may address misconceptions, bridge gaps or extend learning and can take place at any point during the unit.

In addition, cross-curricular links are suggested, including links to challenges from the Learning Challenge Curriculum.

Possible Written Outcomes or Incidental Writing Opportunities

- Prequel - how did the Lost Thing get to the beach? (use action description and dialogue)
- Write in role as the Lost Thing recounting events to the other lost things (Use action, description and dialogue)
- Use Comic Life to create a comic strip version of story either with new character or new Lost Thing
- Children become main character and write the story of their own Lost Thing
- Write a dialogue or play script of a conversation between you and your parents to explain about your Lost Thing
- Non-chronological report about a lost thing
- For sale notice for a lost thing
- Newspaper report on the appearance and disappearance of the Lost Thing
- Discussion - Should the boy help the Lost Thing to find a new home?

YEAR 5 AND 6

Hook

- Show opening of the film The Lost Thing
- Copy and make postcard from book blurb and present to children

1. Responding to the Text

- Visual literacy: Use image of the Lost Thing? What could it be? Why is it lost? Where did it come from?
- Book talk: Look at the first 2 pages. What do we find out about the boy, his life and the world he is living in? Look at the end pages of the bottle top collection. What else can we find out?
- Visual literacy: Explore and annotate as many pages as required and add to understanding of character's life and setting
- Book talk: Does the book raise any questions?
- Book talk: Why do you think people do not notice the Lost Thing?
- Writer talk: Shaun Tan uses text and pictures to tell the story. Can you find examples of how pictures represent paragraphs and how he links ideas from page to page?
- Writer talk: Can you find how the writer uses action, description and dialogue to tell the reader about the boy?
- Writer talk: Spot the punctuation and how it contributes to meaning

2. Capturing Ideas

- Role on the wall for the boy
- Devise questions to ask the boy and hot seat him
- Single bubble activity to capture the setting
- Interview people from the different settings - beach, street, boy's home
- Box up or plot the main events of the story on to a story mountain
- Create a new Lost Thing
- Role play trying to explain to your parents about your Lost Thing
- From the illustration of all the lost things choose a thing to describe and annotate picture - appearance and what it does or is used for
- Present the description to a partner or a group in full sentences
- Create a new character to find the Lost Thing - appearance, interests, thoughts
- Create a soundscape for the story
- Conscience alley - should the boy help the Lost Thing find a home?

Sentence Games (use throughout unit)

- Sentence starter game
- Complex sentence game
- Playing with punctuation game

Guided Reading Possibilities

- Explore book and illustrations focusing on inferring layers of meaning, how the story is moved forward by the paragraphing structure
- Read other books by Shaun Tan - The Rabbits, Tales From Outer Suburbia
- Identify and discuss features of text type for final written outcome. Level of text can be pitched at each groups' level, ensuring both access and challenge.

3. Contextualised Grammar Teaching

- Complex sentences, including non-finite subordinate clauses (ing,ed)
- Expanded sentence starters - adverbials, ed, ing starters
- Secure use of comma with both above
- Use of cohesive devices to link paragraphs - adverbials, connecting adverbs etc.

4. Modelled Writing
Shared Writing
Guided Writing
Independent Writing

MAKING LINKS ACROSS THE CURRICULUM

Geography/Science/History

- Industrialisation and city life
-

Maths

- Make a drawing to scale of your Lost Thing design

ICT

- Use Comic Life or Photo story to create comic strip version
- Use Audacity to create sound for story

PSHE

- Explore the idea of loneliness
- Can you be lonely when you are with other people?

Useful links

http://www.youtube.com/watch?v=t1YG7ZXfC6g
www.shauntan.net

Art/DT

- Look at Salvador Dali's paintings and compare to book illustrations
- Design a lost thing

The Learning Challenge
CURRICULUM

Author: Shaun Tan
Publisher: Hacchette Childrens
ISBN: 978-0734403889

Planning for Quality Texts: Journey to Jo'burg

These documents are intended to support the planning of effective literacy units based on high quality picture books. They are not intended to be lesson plans, but offer a menu of possible ideas for teachers to use as starting points to plan for purposeful learning and give pupils reasons for writing as well as the skills they need to write with impact on their reader. They follow a learning sequence:

- a hook to fully engage and interest the children
- responding to reading activities to allow immersion in and exploration of the text, including picture exploration, book and writer talk
- capturing ideas activities which include drama and talk to support understanding of the text and to develop vocabulary, language and ideas for writing
- possibilities for the contextualised teaching of grammar
- sentence games to develop creativity, vocabulary, language and grammar
- links to guided reading
- a range of writing tasks which may be final unit outcomes or incidental opportunities during the unit

Specific mention is made of the writing sequence:

- modelled writing - teacher models the writing process aloud and the decisions writers make about sentences, paragraphs etc to create impact on the reader. This can also include the modelling of planning and spelling strategies.
- shared writing - collaborative composition with discussion and suggestions about what to write and how to write it to create the intended effect. At this point children may write a sentence/s, often in pairs, on whiteboards which are then discussed.
- guided writing - small group sessions based on specific needs of a specific group of children. The session may address misconceptions, bridge gaps or extend learning and can take place at any point during the unit.

In addition, cross-curricular links are suggested, including links to challenges from the Learning Challenge Curriculum.

YEAR 5 AND 6

Possible Written Outcomes or Incidental Writing Opportunities

- Thought bubbles for characters at different points in the story
- Flashback to the "Time of Fire" told from Dumi's point of view
- Letter from Naledi to Grace describing events at the hospital
- Setting description in style of Beverley Naidoo
- Write story from Grace's point of view
- Write alternative ending to story
- Write first chapter in role as Naledi
- Dialogue between Tiro and Naledi following the arrest of the man at the station
- Incident report of scene at station by policeman
- Report/explanation of Apartheid
- Biography of Nelson Mandela
- Biography/information about Beverley Naidoo and why she wrote Journey to Jo'burg
- Diary entry in role as Naledi with flashback
- Letter from Tiro to Nono, describing the journey
- Summarise the story, noting the key events
- Poem on freedom

Hook

- Clip of Nelson Mandela speaking
- Footage of segregation in South Africa
- Read Chapter 7 up to "Mma stifled her sobs." Predict what the story might be about and when and where it might be set.

1. Responding to the Text

- Book talk: what questions do you have about the story? Does it remind you of any current issues?
- Role on the wall for all main characters - annotate as text is read
- Book talk: why did the children decide to walk to Jo'burg?
- Hot seat Naledi at key points. What dilemmas does she face? What do we learn about her character?
- Book talk: why was the journey so difficult?
- Book talk: why do you think the writer called the last chapter is called "Hope"?
- Book talk: what are the themes in the book?(love, courage, freedom, equality)
- Book talk: find the clues which tell us the book is set in another culture. How do these help us to find the themes?
- Writer talk: how does the writer make the characters so believable?
- Writer talk: Do you think Naledi has been on more than one kind of journey? How does the writer show this?
- Writer talk: what techniques does the writer use through the book to keep the reader engaged?

2. Capturing Ideas

- Story map of key events and characters.
- Identify some key events and characters involved. Do all the events have the same significance for all characters? Use grid to note different thoughts and feelings.
- Conscience alley - should the children go to Jo'burg on their own?
- Debate - Should everyone have identity cards?
- What does freedom mean? What can you do when you have freedom? How do you feel when you have freedom? Mind map
- Role play key scenes and freeze frame
- Develop role play on white only bus as children get on. Freeze frame and thought track.
- Telephone call from Naledi to Grace explaining what happened after they said goodbye
- Research Nelson Mandela and apartheid. Organise key information under headings.
- Revisit initial predictions

Sentence Games (use throughout unit)

- Personification game using abstract nouns - freedom, courage etc
- Experiment with different sentence starters - ing, ed, adverbials
- Add detail to basic sentence - focus on relative clause
- Improve a sentence- focus on the grammatical elements that need consolidation or review

Guided Reading Possibilities

- Other Beverley Naidoo books. Deeper exploration of Journey to Jo'burg
- A Long Walk to Freedom by Nelson Mandela(children's version)
- Identify and discuss features of text type for final written outcome. Level of text can be pitched at each groups' level, ensuring both access and challenge.

3. Contextualised Grammar Teaching

- Poetic sentences drawing on expanded noun phrases, simile, metaphor and personification
- Using modal verbs to argue a point
- Different effect of using first or third person in recounting an event
- Relative clauses to add additional information

4. Modelled Writing
Shared Writing
Guided Writing
Independent Writing

MAKING LINKS ACROSS THE CURRICULUM

Geography/Maths
- Plot the journey on a map
- How far was it? How long would it take to walk?
- Plan alternative ways to undertake the journey. How long would it take by car, by train? How much Would the journeys cost?

History
- Research apartheid
- Nelson Mandela and his role in the changes that took place in South Africa

ICT
- Research information, images and footage related to apartheid
- Create montage with captions using Photo Story or Animoto

PSHE
- Are there examples of prejudice and inequality in our current lives?
- Nelson Mandela's autobiography is called "A Long Walk to Freedom". Why do you think he chose this title?
- What does freedom mean to you?

Useful links
http://edse4212authorstudy.blogspot.ch/2010/12/video-clip-beverley-naidoo-on-journey.html
http://www.bbc.co.uk/history/people/nelson_mandela

Art
- Landscapes - African scenes using different materials to create a collage showing tone and shape and capturing the emotion of Naledi's and Tiro's journey

Year 6 History: Why should the world be ashamed of slavery?

The Learning Challenge CURRICULUM

Author: Beverley Naidoo
Publisher: Harper Collins
ISBN: 978-0-00-726350-9

Planning with Quality Texts: Way Home

These documents are intended to support the planning of effective literacy units based on high quality picture books. They are not intended to be lesson plans, but offer a menu of possible ideas for teachers to use as starting points to plan for purposeful learning and give pupils reasons for writing as well as the skills they need to write with impact on their reader. They follow a learning sequence:

- a hook to fully engage and interest the children
- responding to reading activities to allow immersion in and exploration of the text, including picture exploration, book and writer talk
- capturing ideas activities which include drama and talk to support understanding of the text and to develop vocabulary, language and ideas for writing
- possibilities for the contextualised teaching of grammar
- sentence games to develop creativity, vocabulary, language and grammar
- links to guided reading
- a range of writing tasks which may be final unit outcomes or incidental opportunities during the unit

Specific mention is made of the writing sequence:

- modelled writing - teacher models the writing process aloud and the decisions writers make about sentences, paragraphs etc to create impact on the reader. This can also include the modelling of planning and spelling strategies.
- shared writing - collaborative composition with discussion and suggestions about what to write and how to write it to create the intended effect. At this point children may write a sentence/s, often in pairs, on whiteboards which are then discussed.
- guided writing - small group sessions based on specific needs of a specific group of children. The session may address misconceptions, bridge gaps or extend learning and can take place at any point during the unit.

In addition, cross-curricular links are suggested, including links to challenges from the Learning Challenge Curriculum.

Possible Written Outcomes or Incidental Writing Opportunities

- Writing in role as Shane - diary entries at key points
- Writing in role as Shane - letter home
- Retell event/s from cat's point of view
- Prequel - before Shane left home
- Sequel
- Thought bubbles/speech bubbles at key points
- Balanced argument - Home is always the best place to be
- Response from Agony Aunt
- Letter to Shane to persuade him to go home
- Newspaper report on Shane's disappearance
- Non-chronological report on homelessness and young people
- Poem based on cat, using names and information developed

YEAR 5 AND 6

Hook

- Posters and graffiti around classroom using symbols from book
- "News report" about missing boy
- Missing poster

Sentence Games (use throughout unit)

- Complex sentence game - based on sentence related to text
- Capture a picture - verb/adverb/exclamation/complex sentence followed by a short, punchy sentence
- Conjunctions game - 2 pictures and identified conjunctions to create sentences. Relate to specific text type; debate, persuasion etc
- Varying sentence openings - one word, adverbial phrase of time/place/manner, ed/ing clause etc

Improve a sentence - focus on the grammatical elements that need consolidation or review

Guided Reading Possibilities

- Stories about homelessness: Invisible Girl by Kate Maryon, Street Child by Berlie Doherty
- Non-fiction texts: Life on the Streets by Kaye Stearman
- Identify and discuss features of text type for final written outcome. Level of text can be pitched at each groups' level, ensuring both access and challenge.

1. Responding to the Text

- **Book talk:** Read sections of story and stop to allow pupils to make possible predictions
- **Book talk:** What do you like/dislike about the book? Are there any puzzles or reminders in the book?
- **Book talk:** The author uses different names for the cat. Why? What is the effect?
- **Picture exploration:** Use first double page. What is the setting? What kind of place is it? Does it remind you of anything? The page is ripped - is it the picture or the text which is torn?
- **Picture exploration:** In groups look at different illustrations. Think about and record thoughts and impressions. Feed back ideas to class.
- **Picture exploration:** Use different pictures and "turn the volume up". What would you hear?
- **Picture exploration:** How does the artist use colour and detail to create impact and give us information? How does he use images as symbols?
- **Writer talk:** The text is written in the present tense. What is the effect of this?
- **Writer talk:** In groups/pairs look at sections of text and how author uses different sentence types, use of speech and hidden information to create impact on the reader

2. Capturing Ideas

- In groups, take sections of text and identify information about Shane to develop character profile
- Look at symbols - what do they tell us about Shane? What symbols might represent themselves?
- Map key events
- Freeze frame key events and thought track
- Conscience Alley - should Shane have fought the gang? Should he have left home?
- Debate - Home is always the best place to be
- Hot seat Shane - focus on why he left home and is living on the streets
- Agony aunt - should Shane go home?
- Back to back phone call to parent/sibling
- Role play interview with Shane's parents/siblings. Could be filmed and evaluated for use of language

Develop ideas for the names for the cat. Add additional information - words, phrases, clauses

3. Contextualised Grammar Teaching

- Use of varied sentence types, including the power of three in sentences
- Use of relative clauses to add information
- Use of drop in phrases/clauses to add information

4. Modelled Writing
Shared Writing
Guided Writing
Independent Writing

MAKING LINKS ACROSS THE CURRICULUM

History/Geography
- Living in London or any other major city
- Compare living on the streets in UK with other countries
- Compare living on the streets with Victorian life

Art
- Use illustrator's techniques to create pictures - torn paper and colour range

Useful links
- http://www.railwaychildren.org.uk/our-solution/where-wework/uk/?gclid=CMmMgOv8pLkCFUXJtAodTRMAkQ#.UiB10DbCam5
- http://news.bbc.co.uk/cbbcnews/hi/static/find_out/specials/newsround_extra/russia/html/default.stm

PSHE
- Investigate homelessness in young people and consider reasons
- Discuss gangs and reasons why young people belong to them.

The Learning Challenge
CURRICULUM

Author: Libby Hathorn
Publisher: Anderson Press Ltd
ISBN: 1-84270-232-7

Planning for Quality Texts: The Spider and the Fly

These documents are intended to support the planning of effective literacy units based on high quality picture books. They are not intended to be lesson plans, but offer a menu of possible ideas for teachers to use as starting points to plan for purposeful learning and give pupils reasons for writing as well as the skills they need to write with impact on their reader. They follow a learning sequence:

- a hook to fully engage and interest the children
- responding to reading activities to allow immersion in and exploration of the text, including picture exploration, book and writer talk
- capturing ideas activities which include drama and talk to support understanding of the text and to develop vocabulary, language and ideas for writing
- possibilities for the contextualised teaching of grammar
- sentence games to develop creativity, vocabulary, language and grammar
- links to guided reading
- a range of writing tasks which may be final unit outcomes or incidental opportunities during the unit

Specific mention is made of the writing sequence:

- modelled writing - teacher models the writing process aloud and the decisions writers make about sentences, paragraphs etc to create impact on the reader. This can also include the modelling of planning and spelling strategies.
- shared writing - collaborative composition with discussion and suggestions about what to write and how to write it to create the intended effect. At this point children may write a sentence/s, often in pairs, on whiteboards which are then discussed.
- guided writing - small group sessions based on specific needs of a specific group of children. The session may address misconceptions, bridge gaps or extend learning and can take place at any point during the unit.

In addition, cross-curricular links are suggested, including links to challenges from the Learning Challenge Curriculum.

Possible Written Outcomes or Incidental Writing Opportunities

- Narrative – tell the story of another insect's demise with different flaw
- Different cautionary tale
- Letter in response to spider's letter
- Write a persuasive letter to fly or spider after fly leaves initially
- Explanation texts - How to Be Charming and Get Your Own Way
- Non chronological report on a predator
- Persuasive report – Spiders are great!
- Journalistic writing with bias– the Spider Chronicle or The Fly Times
- Balanced argument - Spider is in the dock – speech for the opposition and prosecution
- First person account
- Character description
- Flashback to another insect's experience
- Dialogue between ghosts
- Play script

YEAR 5 AND 6

Hook

- Wool or string used to make giant web in classroom

1. Responding to the Text

- Book talk: the book is in black and white. Why do you think the writer made that decision?
- Book talk: how do the representations of the insects compare/contrast with our own ideas of them?
- Visual literacy: what do you notice about the web on the pages of dialogue as you go through the book? Why did the author decide to do this?
- Visual literacy: listen to the reading of the poem. What impact do the illustrations add? Listen to the illustrator talking about the book. Has he been successful?
- Visual literacy: the text is represented in a 'silent movie' style. What is the effect of this?
- Book talk: what is the purpose and audience of the letter at the end?
- Book talk: what fiction genre does this book belong to? How do you know?
- Writer talk: look at the persuasive techniques, words and body language. How effective are these and why?
- Writer talk: how has the writer created tension? Identify the techniques and create a toolkit to use in own writing

2. Capturing Ideas

- Capture pages in complex sentences
- Capture pages in 3 verbs and 3 adverbs
- Generate vocabulary/post it notes
- The unspoken dialogue – the ghosts. Role play scenes between the ghost insects.
- Oral retell of ghost insect's experience
- Interview the spider and/or the 'ghost of the fly'
- Consider the characteristics and actions of the spider and the fly. What differences are there? What similarities?
- Debate - Spiders are useful creatures
- Investigate the message – cautionary tales
- Research spiders. Skim, scan and text mark for key information. Collate and organise information.
- Top Trumps game
- Perform sections of text using volume, tone, facial expression and body language to engage the listener
- What is the moral of the story?

Sentence Games (use throughout unit)

- Persuasive sentence starter game - use language to form short spoken argument
- complex sentence game
- Lists game - 5 things in the spider's kitchen, 5 things in the fly's handbag etc.
- Improve a sentence- focus on the grammatical elements that need consolidation or review

Guided Reading Possibilities

- Other cautionary tales - Matilda by Hilaire Belloc
- Non-fiction texts on spiders and insects
- Identify and discuss features of text type for final written outcome. Level of text can be pitched at each groups' level, ensuring both access and challenge.

3. Contextualised Grammar Teaching

- Choice of verbs and adverbs to convey setting and character
- Use different modal verbs to position an argument
- Vary sentence length for impact and effect

4. Modelled Writing
Shared Writing
Guided Writing
Independent Writing

MAKING LINKS ACROSS THE CURRICULUM

Geography/Science
- Research different spiders and their habitats
- Food chains, interdependence and the spider's role

History/ICT/Drama/Music
- Look at other silent movies. Create short sequence and film in black and white. Add music to film.

PSHE
- The book has a clear moral. What can be learned?
- The fly knew that she was in danger, but was lured by the spider appealing to her vanity. How can our characteristics sometimes affect the way we behave?

Useful links
http://www.youtube.com/watch?v=37uYq10YpKY
http://www.teachingbooks.net/author_collection.cgi?id=15&a=1

Art

The Learning Challenge
CURRICULUM

Author: Tony DiTerlizzi
Publisher: Simon and Schuster
ISBN: 978-0-74347-817-5

Planning with Quality Texts: The Boy, The Bear, The Baron, The Bard

These documents are intended to support the planning of effective literacy units based on high quality picture books. They are not intended to be lesson plans, but offer a menu of possible ideas for teachers to use as starting points to plan for purposeful learning and give pupils reasons for writing as well as the skills they need to write with impact on their reader. They follow a learning sequence:

- a hook to fully engage and interest the children
- responding to reading activities to allow immersion in and exploration of the text, including picture exploration, book and writer talk
- capturing ideas activities which include drama and talk to support understanding of the text and to develop vocabulary, language and ideas for writing
- possibilities for the contextualised teaching of grammar
- sentence games to develop creativity, vocabulary, language and grammar
- links to guided reading
- a range of writing tasks which may be final unit outcomes or incidental opportunities during the unit

Specific mention is made of the writing sequence:

- modelled writing - teacher models the writing process aloud and the decisions writers make about sentences, paragraphs etc to create impact on the reader. This can also include the modelling of planning and spelling strategies.
- shared writing - collaborative composition with discussion and suggestions about what to write and how to write it to create the intended effect. At this point children may write a sentence/s, often in pairs, on whiteboards which are then discussed.
- guided writing - small group sessions based on specific needs of a specific group of children. The session may address misconceptions, bridge gaps or extend learning and can take place at any point during the unit.

In addition, cross-curricular links are suggested, including links to challenges from the Learning Challenge Curriculum.

Possible Written Outcomes or Incidental Writing Opportunities

- Write a narrative for the book
- Add speech bubbles and text captions to a section of the book
- Dialogue between two characters which shows their characteristics/personalities
- Description of settings
- Ending for the book with bear or boy as the focus
- Newspaper report looking at bias - towards the Bard and towards the bear and the boy
- Use Comic Life to create additional episode in story
- Use illustrations in a powerpoint and add a voiceover in the style of a commentary
- Discussion - Pictures speak louder than words.

YEAR 6

Hook

- Visit to Globe theatre
- Shakespeare workshop

(Linked to History on Shakespearean England - children need background knowledge about the period.)

1. Responding to the Text

- Use picture on front cover - what impression does the front cover give? Are any of the characters recognisable?
- Within book are there other recognisable characters or features of Shakespearean life?
- Are there any puzzles or reminders in the book?
- Why has Gregory Rogers used different sized pictures? What is the effect of this? What might written text look like?
- Some of the pictures are drawn from different angles. What is the effect of this?
- Identify the themes which run through the book - friendship (clasped hands), escaping from danger(face peering out during chases), good v evil etc
- How do the pictures help us to understand the characters? What do we know about them?
- Look at the end papers. What do they tell us?
- How has Gregory Rogers used colour? What is the effect of this use?

2. Capturing Ideas

- Role play different scenes
- Freeze frame and thought track the different characters
- Role play dialogue between two characters
- Build a toolkit for an adventure story
- Watch clips of TV interviews and identify questions and language used for responses
- Role play/and film interview of different characters. Evaluate effectiveness of questioning and use of language
- Look at how the pictures quicken and slow pace - collect words and phrases and techniques that will support different paces in written text
- Look at larger illustrations of settings and annotate with nouns, develop into noun phrases, add to annotations with verbs and adverbs and adverbial phrases
- Debate - Pictures speak louder than words. Identify discursive language required and evaluate its use

Sentence Games (use throughout unit)

- Capture the picture - in an exclamation, in a sound effect, in a complex sentence
- Use two of the pictures or characters and a choice of conjunctions to develop sentences and discuss effect
- Play with different sentence starters - adjective, ing, ed, adverbial
- Improve a sentence - focus on the grammatical elements that need consolidation or review

Guided Reading Possibilities

- Read other graphic books and compare to The Boy, the Bear, the Baron and the Bard
- Shakespearean stories either as text or in graphic novel form
- Identify and discuss features of text type for final written outcome. Level of text can be pitched at each groups' level, ensuring both access and challenge.

3. Contextualised Grammar Teaching

- Use of expanded noun phrases to add detail
- Use of adverbials to vary writing
- Use of range of sentence types to control and create an effect on the reader - an adverbial starter, a complex sentence, one word, short sentence etc. Experiment with and make choices for impact.

4. Modelled Writing
Shared Writing
Guided Writing
Independent Writing

MAKING LINKS ACROSS THE CURRICULUM

History
- Most links within learning challenge
- Research a banquet, prepare food and hold banquet

PSHE
- The bear was being held in a cage. This was common then. Are animals still ill-treated in this way?(Charles Causley's poem - My Mother Saw a Dancing Bear)
- What would life have been like for the boy if he had remained in Elizabethan England? Now, all children have the right to an education. Would that have been the case then?

Music/Dance
- Research and listen to Elizabethan music
- Research and perform an Elizabethan dance

Art/ICT
- Create comic strip, carefully considering the sizing of each section
- Experiment with different colour palettes and the impact

Useful links
- http://www.globe-theatre.org.uk/
- http://www.rsc.org.uk/education/resources/

Year 6 History:
To be or not to be, that is the question?

The Learning Challenge
CURRICULUM

Author: Gregory Rogers
Publisher: Roaring Brook Press
ISBN: 978-1596430099

Planning with Quality Texts: The Watertower

These documents are intended to support the planning of effective literacy units based on high quality picture books. They are not intended to be lesson plans, but offer a menu of possible ideas for teachers to use as starting points to plan for purposeful learning and give pupils reasons for writing as well as the skills they need to write with impact on their reader. They follow a learning sequence:

- a hook to fully engage and interest the children
- responding to reading activities to allow immersion in and exploration of the text, including picture exploration, book and writer talk
- capturing ideas activities which include drama and talk to support understanding of the text and to develop vocabulary, language and ideas for writing
- possibilities for the contextualised teaching of grammar
- sentence games to develop creativity, vocabulary, language and grammar
- links to guided reading
- a range of writing tasks which may be final unit outcomes or incidental opportunities during the unit

Specific mention is made of the writing sequence:

- modelled writing - teacher models the writing process aloud and the decisions writers make about sentences, paragraphs etc to create impact on the reader. This can also include the modelling of planning and spelling strategies.
- shared writing - collaborative composition with discussion and suggestions about what to write and how to write it to create the intended effect. At this point children may write a sentence/s, often in pairs, on whiteboards which are then discussed.
- guided writing - small group sessions based on specific needs of a specific group of children. The session may address misconceptions, bridge gaps or extend learning and can take place at any point during the unit.

In addition, cross-curricular links are suggested, including links to challenges from the Learning Challenge Curriculum.

Year 6

Possible Written Outcomes or Incidental Writing Opportunities

- Write a narrative for the book
- Write an opening with a fiction hook based on an ordinary but sinister place
- Dialogue between two characters which shows their characteristics/personalities
- Narrative episode showing character's fear through their thoughts
- Write two paragraphs that describe two events occurring at the same time
- Diary entry - Spike or Bubba
- Newspaper report discussing the strange behaviour of the townspeople.
- Letter explaining the situation and persuading the Police Chief to come and investigate
- Write a prequel to the book

Hook

- Use front cover without title. What is this? Where is it? Why is it there?
- Show book trailer clip (See useful links)

1. Responding to the Text

- Read the opening without showing picture. Children visualise and sketch.
- What do you like/dislike about the book?
- Are there any puzzles or reminders in the book?
- Look at the use of colour? What is the effect?
- Some of the pictures are drawn from different angles and are different sizes. What is the effect of this?
- Look at how the text and the pictures show two different events taking place simultaneously.
- Consider how much the text is like a film– are there any similar films the children know of?
- How does Gary Crew use language to develop the characters?
- How does Gary Crew use language to build tension? How does he lull the reader into a false sense of security?
- Consider the unexplained ending of the story. What is the impact of this?
- Role on the wall for Bubba and Spike

2. Capturing Ideas

- Hot seating different towns people
- Freeze frame and thought track the characters at key points
- Compare the two characters
- Interview Bubba before and after his change
- Interview Spike about Bubba's change
- Build a toolkit for a fiction hook opening to a story
- Discuss how the text would need developing if it was not a picture book
- Organise images from the story to represent opening, build-up, problem, resolution, ending.
- Explore the pictures and annotate with words and phrases. Develop to simile and metaphor. Add connecting adverbs and adverbial
- Debate - Alien Invasion? Identify discursive language required and evaluate its use

Sentence Games (use throughout unit)

- Capture the picture - in three adjectives, three verbs/adverbs/a complex sentence
- Image of watertower - create a personality for it. What would it hear, touch, see? What would it think about?
- Play with different sentence starters - adjective, ing, ed, adverbial
- Improve a sentence - focus on the grammatical elements that need consolidation or review

Guided Reading Possibilities

- Use visual literacy techniques to deepen understanding of The Watertower (http://mrscohen2012.files.wordpress.com/2012/02/the-watertower-study-guide-complete.pdf)
- Other horror stories - e.g. Clockwork by Philip Pullman, The Graveyard Book by Neil Gaiman
- Identify and discuss features of text type for final written outcome. Level of text can be pitched at each groups' level, ensuring both access and challenge.

3. Contextualised Grammar Teaching

- Use of expanded noun phrases to add detail
- Use of simile, metaphor and personification
- Use of range of sentence types to control and create an effect on the reader - an adverbial starter, a complex sentence, one word, short sentence etc. Experiment with and make choices for impact.

4. Modelled Writing
Shared Writing
Guided Writing
Independent Writing

MAKING LINKS ACROSS THE CURRICULUM

Geography
- Links within learning challenge
- Research the use of watertowers and other ways of accessing and/or storing water

PSHE
- Was Spike a bully? Relate to other contexts.

ICT/Art
- Make short film sequence using different camera angles to create suspense
- Make a book trailer for another horror story

Useful links
- http://mrscohen2012.files.wordpress.com/2012/02/the-watertower-study-guide-complete.pdf
- http://www.youtube.com/watch?v=nYQOWJ_Zz-o

Science
- Materials and their properties - looking at properties of metals and the reasons for the formation of rust

Year 6 Geography
Will you ever see the water you drink again?

The Learning Challenge CURRICULUM

Author: Gary Crew
Publisher: Crocodile Books USA
ISBN: 978-1566563314

Planning for Quality Texts: How to Train Your Dragon

These documents are intended to support the planning of effective literacy units based on high quality picture books. They are not intended to be lesson plans, but offer a menu of possible ideas for teachers to use as starting points to plan for purposeful learning and give pupils reasons for writing as well as the skills they need to write with impact on their reader. They follow a learning sequence:

- a hook to fully engage and interest the children
- responding to reading activities to allow immersion in and exploration of the text, including picture exploration, book and writer talk
- capturing ideas activities which include drama and talk to support understanding of the text and to develop vocabulary, language and ideas for writing
- possibilities for the contextualised teaching of grammar
- sentence games to develop creativity, vocabulary, language and grammar
- links to guided reading
- a range of writing tasks which may be final unit outcomes or incidental opportunities during the unit

Specific mention is made of the writing sequence:

- modelled writing - teacher models the writing process aloud and the decisions writers make about sentences, paragraphs etc. to create impact on the reader. This can also include the modelling of planning and spelling strategies.
- shared writing - collaborative composition with discussion and suggestions about what to write and how to write it to create the intended effect. At this point children may write a sentence/s, often in pairs, on whiteboards which are then discussed.
- guided writing - small group sessions based on specific needs of a specific group of children. The session may address misconceptions, bridge gaps or extend learning and can take place at any point during the unit.

In addition, cross-curricular links are suggested, including links to challenges from the Learning Challenge Curriculum.